A Warm Place

Young Voices on Faith

compiled and edited by

Heather Cardin

George Ronald
Oxford

George Ronald, *Publisher*
Oxford
www.grbooks.com

© Heather Cardin 2007
All Rights Reserved

*A catalogue record for this book is available
from the British Library*

ISBN 978-0-85398-517-4

A Warm Place in My Heart

This book is dedicated to

Fraser Glen, beloved friend since our youth
&
Lisa Brosseau, dear friend and wise mentor

with love

The youthful and eager workers for the Cause . . . occupy a warm place in my heart. I will remember their hopes, their plans, their activities in my hours of prayer at the Holy Shrine. I urge them to study profoundly the revealed utterances of Bahá'u'lláh and the discourses of 'Abdu'l-Bahá and not to rely unduly on the representation and interpretation of the Teachings given by Bahá'í speakers and teachers.

May the Almighty sustain you and guide you in your work.

Note in the handwriting of Shoghi Effendi, appended to a letter dated 20 March 1929 written on his behalf to an individual

Contents

Acknowledgements	vii
Introduction	x
Amy Tidswell	1
David Fauteux	4
James Farr	6
Kokoro Tabata	8
Kurt Kreuger	9
Harsh Pancholi	11
Hayley Miloff	20
Priscilla Fang	21
Michael Skuce	23
Dona Séléger	24
Eric Michell	26
Ilya Shodjaee-Zrudlo	29
Kira Baskerville	32
Natasha Sinniece Collishaw	34
Tahereh Haji	37
Kai Bighorn	39
Anonymous	43
Chelsea Gifford	47
Daniel Jones	49
Chloë Filson	55
Angus Cowan Epp	56
Luke (Ahkivgak) Baumgartner	57
Nysa Pilbrow	63
Juliette Lord	65
Melodie Cardin	70
Anisa Qualls	74

Matthew Morrissey	88
Tahirih Alia	91
Marzieh Thorne	99
Alexis Nieland	103
Shahnaz Kintz	104
Fei-Lee Leong de Blanco	108
Aletha Phillips	111
Celeste Gómez	112
Thomas Mitchell Doran and Tim Doran	114
Robert Gillies	116
Matt Fillmore	117
Olinga Martel	121
Amelia Dana	134
Omid Khorramian	141
José Silva	144
Edward Robertson	147
Sylvain Hutchison	151
Jesse Harris	154
Bibliography	162

Acknowledgements

This book is clearly a collective endeavour. I am deeply grateful to all of those who took the time, amongst the many I invited, to write and send their reflections, including one woman who prefers to remain unknown for reasons which will be obvious. Thank you:

Tahirih Alia, Kira Baskerville, Luke (Ahkivgak) Baumgartner, Kai Bighorn, Melodie Cardin, Natasha Collishaw, Amelia Dana, Thomas Mitchell Doran, Timothy Doran, Angus Epp, Priscilla Fang, James Farr, David Fauteux, Matt Fillmore, Chloë Filson, Chelsea Gifford, Robert Gillies, Celeste Gómez, Tahereh Haji, Jesse Harris, Sylvain Hutchison, Daniel Jones, Omid Khorramian, Shahnaz Kintz, Kurt Kreuger, Juliette Lord, Fei-Lee Leong de Blanco, Olinga Martel, Eric Michell, Hayley Miloff, Matthew Morrissey, Alexis Nieland, Harsh Pancholi, Aletha Phillips, Nysa Pilbrow, Anisa Qualls, Edward Robertson, Dona (Fanfan) Séléger, Ilya Shodjaee-Zrudlo, José Silva, Michael Skuce, Kokoro Tabata, Marzieh Thorne, Amy Tidswell, Anonymous

Thank you also to the parents of those authors under the age of 18 who have graciously given their permission for their children's essays to appear in this book.

I am also grateful to a number of friends who assisted with various aspects of this work. Regan Roy, from his pioneer post, located two Peruvian youth to contribute to the book, and translated José Silva's contribution from the Spanish. Nozomu Sonda, of the National Spiritual Assembly of the Baháʼís of Japan and a former colleague from Maxwell International Baháʼí School, located the Japanese youth who contributed and translated her contribution from the Japanese. Julie Benoit Séléger translated her husband Fanfan's contribution from the French. Thank you, Regan, Nozomu and Julie.

In order to find youth from different countries who would be willing to contribute, I asked friends near and far to help out. Sandra Fotos, whom I had met while working at Maxwell and whom I knew as a pioneer to Japan, responded quickly to my request for assistance and located Suzanna Kawamura, who forwarded my request to Nozomu Sonda. This was truly teamwork. Ginny Kintz, who had also been a contributor to my first book, *Partners in Spirit: What Couples Say about Marriages that Work*, ensured that her daughter Shahnaz's essay was sent, and Gayle Hoover Thorne of Sacramento sent her daughter Marzieh's reflections on various Bahá'í events. Ho-San and Mariette Leong, who had also contributed to my book on marriage, persevered and encouraged their daughter Fei-Lee to contribute her views, thus giving us a truly international glimpse of how the Bahá'í teachings had affected one young woman from Oceania. Frances Pilbrow invited her daughter Nysa, who invited her close friend Natasha. Cheryl Epp interviewed her son Angus and transcribed his words verbatim. Mae Nieland sent her son Alexis's contribution and Amelia Epp encouraged her friend (and my former student) Anisa Qualls to write to me. Ilya Shodjaee connected me with his friend Jesse Harris. A friend and fellow writer in Ottawa, Jay Howden, connected me with Matt Fillmore in Macau. Our dear family friends Bill and Houri Skuce introduced me to Bill's nephew, Michael, who had just declared his faith in Bahá'u'lláh. Wendi Momen suggested that I contact both Amy Tidswell and Enoch Tanyi, and Enoch contacted Priscilla Fang, giving us a voice from West Africa. Judy Tompkins invited her daughter Kira Baskerville to contribute. My friends Ann and David Hall suggested that I contact the young woman who contributed anonymously, as well as encouraging their daughter Amelia Dana to send her reflections. Jennifer Phillips, who has become a friend through her marriage to my cousin Jack McLean, invited her daughter Aletha to write her thoughts. Hayley Miloff's mother, Helen de Marsh, ensured that Hayley's heartwarming contribution arrived.

My family has continued to encourage me with my writing projects. My husband Bernie is supportive and enthusiastic. Our daughter Melodie is a contributor to the book itself but is also a contributor to every joy in her mother's life. Our daughter Maya and our son Jesse engage me in delightful conversations and remind me of the energy and enthusiasm of youth. All three of our children are precious and deeply loved. I am grateful, always, to my parents, Ron and Edna Nablo, who embraced the Bahá'í teachings in the early 1950s and have modelled love and faith for me, my four sisters and our brother, all of whom have embraced the Bahá'í Faith.

My cousin Jack McLean, a writer and scholar, suggested that I should send this book to Wendi Momen. The result has been a wonderful sense of encouragement, timeliness and Bahá'í unity. I am deeply grateful to all who have assisted in finding these stories of faith, stories of the experiences young people from around the world have had through their practice of faith. I am especially grateful for the courage and honesty of those who so openly shared the stories of their hearts. It is an honour to share their stories with you.

Introduction

Why have faith? Why practise faith in the world as it is today?

In the mid-19th century, a Persian nobleman, later entitled Bahá'u'lláh, announced that He was the messenger of God for this day and age. He claimed to fulfil the prophecies of the religions of the past and to open the door to a future replete with hope and spirituality. He was imprisoned in His homeland, then known in the West as Persia, for these claims and died an exile and a prisoner in 1892. His son, entitled 'Abdu'l-Bahá and designated the 'Centre of His Covenant', carried on Bahá'u'lláh's message. The story of Bahá'u'lláh's life, and that of 'Abdu'l-Bahá, known to Bahá'ís as the Master, occupies several volumes.

In the early part of the 20th century 'Abdu'l-Bahá travelled to carry His father's message to the West, spending a lengthy period of time in Europe, the United States and Canada. He spoke in many cities, was welcomed as a dignitary, proclaimed His message in churches and public halls and was acclaimed as a public speaker in North America from east to west and north to south. Significant among the books available are compilations of His talks and letters, including the series of letters to North American Bahá'ís entitled *The Tablets of the Divine Plan* in which He outlines methods by which the 'healing message' of His father's Faith can be brought to all humanity. In His will, read at His death in 1921, He clearly appointed His own grandson to guard this developing Faith. Shoghi Effendi, designated the Guardian of the Bahá'í Faith, had been educated at Oxford with the express purpose of giving him mastery over the English language. The Guardian tirelessly served the Faith of Bahá'u'lláh until his death in 1957. His primary task had been to establish a method by which this rapidly growing Faith, with its vision of the unity of the world's peoples, could be administered from the grassroots level. In 1963, shortly after Shoghi Effendi's passing, the first Universal House of Justice, the supreme governing body of the Faith envisioned by Bahá'u'lláh, was elected by representatives from the countries of the world.

As the 21st century opened, the Bahá'ís could be found in almost every nation of the world, the Faith enjoying in most esteem and respect. A conspicuous exception was, of course, Iran, where Bahá'ís have been persecuted and put to death for the sake of their beliefs. The importance of the message of this Faith is honoured through its representation as a non-governmental organization at the United Nations, as well as in its inclusion in many symposia and conferences on religious and current affairs. The Bahá'í Faith continues to grow. Beautiful temples have been erected on every continent in the name of the Faith, in which people from all religions are invited to worship.

The Bahá'í Faith has clear social laws and obligations which run counter to many of the social trends in the West. Bahá'ís are forbidden sexual expression outside of the marriage bond. Alcohol and other drugs are prohibited. Daily obligatory prayer is required, and once a year, like their Muslim forebears, Bahá'ís undertake a fast for spiritual renewal and cleansing. Bahá'ís are not allowed to take part in partisan politics, nor are they permitted to gamble, cheat at business or lie. Setbacks in these areas are viewed with mercy and love; it is understood that the spiritual path is one of process, not necessarily a quick arrival at a destination, but the belief is that people can, and will, transform themselves for the sake of their love of God.

The Faith grows. Its adherents come from all walks of life, from all over the world and from every culture, every religious background and every language group. People choose to become Bahá'ís every day. It is not an easy choice, nor are Bahá'ís expected to attain perfection. What Bahá'ís are expected to do is to try, very hard, to integrate the spiritual admonitions of the Founder of the Faith into their daily lives. They believe, completely, that the God they follow is the same God who has given guidance from time immemorial. Bahá'ís embrace fellowship with people of Hindu,

Muslim, Christian, Sikh, Buddhist, Zoroastrian, First Nations and Jewish beliefs, as well as those who are followers of many other systems, or of none. The primary goal is unity with the peoples of the world, encompassing the rich diversity of peoples and cultures, the elimination of prejudices in all its forms and the embrace of spiritually-based moral values.

These beliefs can seem utopian, naive and anachronistic; they can equally inspire, encourage and bring hope for the future. People are encouraged to investigate the Bahá'í teachings independently; there is no coercion to convert. If people find that Bahá'u'lláh's claims are true, then they become Bahá'ís and 'little by little, day by day' they practise their Faith, share it with those interested and hope for the unity of humanity in which they believe.

Why believe in a faith and why practise its beliefs?

These are questions which interested me. I was raised by parents who declared their acceptance of the Bahá'í Faith, from their respective Christian denominations, in the early 1950s. My first travel for the Bahá'í Faith was to an international conference held in Iceland when I was about to turn 15. I have since travelled to several countries in which it has been my pleasure to meet, and to teach, people from every religious background. With my husband of over 20 years, I am the parent of three wonderful young adults. Professionally, I have been a teacher in high school systems all of my adult life and now devote myself to writing and, currently, to a university position as an instructor. Four of my years in education were spent at one of the several schools inspired by the Bahá'í teachings, Maxwell International Bahá'í School, on Vancouver Island in Canada.

Many of the young people I encountered there, and in communities around the globe, are people who choose to believe in God and to practise their faith. Many of their friends also believe; they are committed to a spiritual path. They are neither indoctrinated nor do they believe through blind faith. They choose to practise religion with joy, volition and, sometimes, considerable struggle. Their beliefs go against the grain of most of 'pop culture'. Not all children from Bahá'í families choose the Bahá'í Faith but many do. They serve their chosen faith through socioeconomic development projects, by educating themselves in fields of endeavour where they can offer service to humanity without consideration of significant financial reward or simply by choosing to sacrifice more popular aspects of the culture for the sake of spiritual pursuits. Others, not from Bahá'í families, elect to become Bahá'ís because they encounter the hope these teachings offer in a time which can otherwise seem hopeless. Some of those who wrote about their faith for this book continue to have a roller-coaster ride of faith but all know the deep importance of their faith in their lives.

Why? What makes a young person in the early part of the 21st century willing to follow a Faith that requires exemplary moral conduct and which views spiritual growth as the purpose of an otherwise very material life?

This is the question I asked young people. I invited Bahá'í youth and young adults to share their thoughts about why they believed and why they were Bahá'ís. I was pleased to hear from young people in a variety of countries, although most who responded were from North America. I was interested in their challenges and their successes, their reflections, their experiences, their hopes and dreams. I was blessed by already having many friends amongst young people, several of whom I had met as their teacher at Maxwell School. Loving bonds had been established which continue to enrich my life and those of my peers, colleagues and other friends of my own generation. I will always be grateful for the mentorship my own daughter received from the teachers at that extraordinary school, especially from my close friend Lisa Brosseau, one of the two dear friends to whom this book is dedicated.

I should note that, occasionally, you will encounter 'Bahá'í' terminology. While Bahá'ís do not have paid clergy or missionaries, we do have a programme of 'pioneering', whereby people leave their community of origin to assist the growth of Bahá'í communities in other locales. These believers are designated 'pioneers'. Currently, a specific form of workshop training, covering many of the basic Bahá'í writings and directed to the development of the Bahá'í community, called the 'Ruhi' institute is being followed by many Bahá'ís. Thus several of the writers refer to their participation in these institutes, making mention of study circles or particular books in the sequence of courses they are following. Others refer to 'deepening', which simply means studying the Baháʾí scriptures and teachings. The various administrative forms of local, national and international government are referred to: these are the Spiritual Assemblies and the Universal House of Justice, which has its seat in Haifa, Israel, which Baháʾís consider the Holy Land. A couple of the young people have written their narratives while contributing their skills to the Baháʾí World Centre in the Holy Land in 'a year of service'. A year of service, in fact, is simply that: an interim year, sometimes a little more or less, in which a person will volunteer to assist a Baháʾí community in its growth for a particular period of time. At the World Centre there is much to do to maintain the beauty of the environment, assist with scholarship, research the history and assist with the administrative work.

The individuals who have responded to my question, 'Why are you a Baháʾí?' range in age from about 13 to 30. They answered the questions with depth, caring and passion. Their voices come to you here 'live'. I have edited only for small grammatical details. My daughter told me that adults often get young voices wrong. For this reason, I wanted these stories to come to you as they are. Here are the voices of young Baháʾís about why they are Baháʾís, why they believe and who they are. I hope you are as heartened by them as I am and will understand, with Shoghi Effendi, the Guardian of our Faith, why they continue to 'occupy a warm place in my heart'.

Amy Tidswell

Amy was born in London, England, in 1987 to a Persian Bahá'í mother and a British father. Her parents divorced and she was raised by her mother, who died when Amy was 11. She was adopted by a Bahá'í family and at 16 pioneered with her family to Bulgaria, attending a Bahá'í private school, Townshend International School, in the Czech Republic. In October 2005 she began a year of service in Brno, Czech Republic, and will eventually go to university to study her passions, English and Education. She loves music, dancing, and travelling and wants to be privileged to bring spiritual education to children.

I always love to hear how people became Bahá'ís and about the journey they travelled before they found the Faith. It's something so sacred, so special, and being born into a Bahá'í family, I feel I missed something. Somehow I missed the *thrill of the chase*! I have always known the Faith and had the privilege of having it handed to me on a plate, being surrounded by the writings and Bahá'í community as I've grown up, so it's all natural to me. I never had this moment of *I've found it* – it has always been normal, natural and just logical for me. Of course there is a wisdom in every design of the universe and I thank God regularly that I was born into a Bahá'í family because God knows whether I would have been the type of person to find the Faith by myself! But saying all of that, I *do* find the Faith every day in the little confirmations I receive around me. Whether it's the buzz of excitement when I mention Bahá'u'lláh's name to a seeker or the spiritual dimension in a special friendship that just can't be put into words, I feel the spirit of faith growing stronger every time I *find* it.

I was born into a Bahá'í family, my mother being a Persian Bahá'í and my parents divorcing when I was a young child. All I can remember are stories of Bahá'u'lláh and memorizing prayers and God being a really big part of my life, even day to day. As a junior youth I participated in many weekend deepenings and conferences, which now I see was a huge factor in the strengthening of my Bahá'í identity. I'm sure that's the main reason why I am a Bahá'í now and didn't drift from the Faith. All things that were, and are, dearest to me are connected to the Faith somehow. I had, and have, so many close friends, but spiritually close, which is a closeness that will last through all worlds, that creates an atmosphere of positive peer pressure. And, of course, there has definitely been intervention from the Abhá Kingdom, directing me and guiding me throughout.

Before my mother's passing I had been thoroughly deepened on the subject of life after death, the will of God and the purpose of our existence. It not only prepared me for her departure from this world but grounded in me a deep love and understanding of this Faith of ours. I attached myself to the thing that connected me to her, Bahá'u'lláh.

At this point I recall a short experience I had recently.

This last summer I was visiting my hometown in England – Colchester – and was having a conversation in the car with one of my friends, who is not a Bahá'í, about our future plans for studying. At some point I innocently asked how he was going to change the world.

He gave me a confused look, so I tried to clarify and asked him, 'What are you going to do to make the world a better place? Where is your place in the whole scheme of the world?'

However, his confused look persisted. He shrugged his shoulders. 'I don't want to. I'm not going to.'

I insisted and with an impatient tone asked him, 'BUT WHAT ARE YOU GOING TO DO?'

He replied, 'I don't know!' in a tone that implied I was asking the oddest question.

For me, it was the most normal question. For me, it's logical. In this world none of us is alone. It's clear that where the world is going is not right. Everyone must do something to change the world and everyone can. Everyone has their place, their niche and can do whatever they can. My friend didn't agree though.

'I can't do anything,' he said.

That was it. It set me off.

'BUT YOU CAN! EVERYONE CAN DO SOMETHING! WE CAN'T JUST LIVE IN THE WORLD AND TAKE BUT NOT GIVE!'

The passion with which these words were screeched made him laugh.

'OK, OK, I'll give to charity, I'll give to a good cause.'

That conversation, though brief and without a conclusion, so to speak, was a huge eye-opener for me. It was then that I realized exactly why I am a Bahá'í in this day. It is not like joining a religion. Becoming a Bahá'í is realizing the eternal, changeless Faith of God – that all religions are not equal but are one. And it is more than joining an organization that tries to do good for the world – there are many such organizations. But it is a group of people who have realized their spiritual essence and are trying to carry out the will of God on earth. It may seem a bold statement but I believe everybody has their place in the Bahá'í Faith. Everybody has something different that connects them to the Faith. Bahá'u'lláh, the fulfilment of all prophecies, has come and actually given the remedy for the world's problems. We don't even need to find the solutions! They are ready! We only have to carry out the work. It lies on our shoulders to fulfil the tasks.

That is why I am a Bahá'í. I cannot know of such truths and not try my utmost to act on them. I am so convinced that the new world order that Bahá'u'lláh has brought for us will function and bring about world peace so dearly desired by all, Muslims, Christians, Jews, Buddhists alike and non-believers too, that I feel the greatest service I can give to the world is to promote Bahá'u'lláh's message, His principles and teachings, to whoever wants to hear them.

The story with my friend serves as a reminder to me how many people really don't know their place in the world and don't know their great capacities, their great destinies. The despair in those words of his, the acceptance of the world as it is, the belief that world peace is not possible is sadly common in our world today.

All my questions and problems are answered in the writings of the Faith. And if not specifically, we have the guidance of our divinely ordained institutions. All my strength and motivation comes from God and my connection to him through Bahá'u'lláh. A friend asked me the other day, 'Why are you so happy? What do you have?'

Through all the tests I have been given, the one solid rock, the surest thing I have, is God. I know He is always with me and will never cease to be with me. It is God who will give me anything I really need, it is He who will be my eternal companion. Sounds rather like a love story. In fact it is. It is a love story with no ending. I will never attain the goal but will continually seek the Beloved throughout eternity. How would I know what I am in reality without Bahá'u'lláh's teachings? Without God telling me, through His Manifestation? I wouldn't really be living at all! For me, being a Bahá'í is a great gift but also a grave responsibility and not one we have been given by chance. And we only have one chance. We have no other choice but to seize it. If this is our responsibility, the best way I can fulfil my part is by dedicating myself to the cause of Bahá'u'lláh and, thus, call myself 'Bahá'í'.

David Fauteux

Born in 1980, David Fauteux was raised in a middle-class family whose parents managed to impart many important values to their son. His happy childhood was unfortunately followed by teenage years fraught with pain and disappointment. He was introduced to the Bahá'í Faith by his best friend's mother. From 16 to 20 he attended 'firesides' at a local Bahá'í centre, where he learned a great deal about the Faith and spirituality. At 20 he chose to accept Bahá'u'lláh in his heart. He has been Bahá'í for six years.

Bahá'ís who were not raised in Bahá'í families will often recount that they knew in their hearts that they had been Bahá'í all their lives. Essentially, through our introduction to the Faith, we come to understand the true meaning of the longing we have felt in our hearts for many years.

I am no different. I was raised in a typical North American family. My parents did not practise any particular religious tradition. I was not baptized, we did not go to church and the family Bible was a dusty book on a shelf in the basement library. Nothing in my environment, at that age, would point to me becoming a religious person.

However, I was definitely spiritual, though I could not have articulated it as definitely and distinctly then as I can now. At the time, it was nothing more than a vague impression that someone was watching over me, that there was more to life than the daily grind. It was not until I was introduced to the Bahá'í Faith and eventually came to accept Bahá'u'lláh that I fully grasped the significance of what I had found: God had been guiding my way all along. By the grace of God, the ship that was in my heart had finally come to port.

Ever since my recognition of Bahá'u'lláh as God's divine messenger for this age my life has had a purpose. If I follow His guidance and remain steadfast throughout my time on earth, I may be able to attain, in the afterlife, the presence of my beloved God. This may sound farfetched to some while others may see it as a gamble that is hardly worth it, especially in this age devoid of meaning, but to me it is a real and powerful force in my life.

Without purpose, my life was aimless, sad and lonely. I longed for intimacy, for a true spiritual connection. I wanted to be loved unconditionally and I wanted to love unconditionally. Regrettably, after so many disappointments, my hope began to fade. I became very lonely and solitary. *Why depend on others if I was only going to be let down?* Fortunately, by the time I began to entertain these thoughts, I had found Bahá'u'lláh.

He taught me that I was a noble creature worthy of God's love; that the difficulties we encounter in life are meant to make us stronger and bring us closer to our Beloved; that I could contribute to the betterment of the world through service to humanity.

What a contrast – it was not very difficult to choose to pursue the avenue of faith further. Over the years, as I grew spiritually, I came to integrate many things into my life. I stopped worrying about things that were out of my control. If I fell, God would catch me. I came to be very patient with people because I realized that they were stumbling through life looking for the key to their hearts, as I had been. I came to love my fellow human beings, not because of anything they did or did not do but because they are all God's beautiful creatures. I gained a desire to help the less fortunate. I give money to charity without reservation, donate blood and collect food for the local food bank. I no longer fear looking deep down inside the recesses of my soul because what was once dark now bathes in light and joy.

This light and joy is, in the end, the true measure of how much I have gained by opening my heart to God's love through Bahá'u'lláh.

James Farr

James Farr is the youngest of three children born to Tom Farr and Deirdre Jackson. His mother has practised the Bahá'í Faith since her youth. James graduated from Philemon Wright High School in 2006 and is currently a student at the Heritage CEGEP college in the Hull sector of Gatineau.

I am a 17 year old Bahá'í youth living in Canada. Although I am constitutionally granted the freedom of religious expression, the extreme decadence that western culture has created for itself is probably the least conducive place for anyone attempting to lead his life in a humble, pious manner. Once young people reach a certain age, society manipulates their naiveté and ravages their youthful energy. If we depend on our culture for enrichment, we effectively lose any chance we had for spiritual growth.

I choose to be a Bahá'í because it seems to me to be the only place where I can find much needed moral nourishment in today's context. Your teenage years are your formative ones, where many of the choices you make mould you into the human you eventually become. The Faith, for me, serves as a compass, reliably directing my decisions to a nobler star. Of course, like anyone else who has accepted Bahá'u'lláh's mission, I've had and still have trials and tests that I must deal with but these never lessen my faith in God.

I'm writing this on a Monday night. I mention this only because Monday is the day when I find out what my friends have done over the weekend. Let that alone stand as a confirmation of why I am living the life of a Bahá'í! The endless cycle of substance abuse and promiscuity that hurts my friends, and me by relation, is enough. The worst of it is that society has misled us into believing that this horrifying lack of moderation is a natural part of growing up! To clear up some misconceptions, when I say 'society', I am not saying that this is some foreign entity. Obviously, youth are a part of society. When we are told that doing drugs and the like is a natural part of being a teenager, we are being told what we want to hear. And this is likely the saddest part of all.

That being said, I always have to remember never to judge the actions of other human beings harshly, for in doing so I undermine the very message of our religion. In judging someone, I suggest that I have a deep comprehension of the existence of that person, which is ridiculous. We are created in the image of God, who is completely beyond our comprehension. Shouldn't that, if nothing else, demonstrate that we'll never have full understanding of another human being? This is one of my hardest struggles, recognizing what is right and wrong but not letting that impede my journey to an all-embracing love of humankind. What I should always remember as well is that while people are so nobly complex, they are also so endearingly simple. And the simplicity really is an endearing attribute because it shows us to be the flawed creation that we all are, and that brings us all to one unified level.

The Bahá'í Faith has been the singularly most influential and vital aspect in my development as a human being. It gives me hope when the wickedness of people oppresses me, it gives me strength when I have been hurt and, most importantly, it gives me a reason for all the suffering and heartache we feel and a reason to push on despite it. By tying myself securely to the Faith, I free myself from the world.

A WARM PLACE IN MY HEART

Kokoro Tabata

Introduction and translation by Nozomu Sonda

Kokoro was born in 1987 in Yamaguchi, Japan, and grew up there. She attended Maxwell International Bahá'í School for one year (2005–6) and graduated from a Japanese high school in March 2006. She currently resides in Japan.

I was born and raised in Yamaguchi, Japan. On 29 March 2005, when I was 17 years old and in the 11th grade at my Japanese high school, I transferred to Maxwell International Bahá'í School in B.C., Canada. One year later (10 February 2006) I returned to Japan, graduating from my original high school because they recognized the credits I earned in Canada.

I was born and raised a Bahá'í, so I had had contact with the Faith even before I became really aware of it. It was when I was in the 9th grade that I began to be conscious of the Faith. I had not even thought about what the Faith was about until then. So when I found out that the Bahá'í Faith was a religion, I was shocked. The Faith gives an impression so different from what is so-called 'religion'.

As I recall the days when I first studied Ruhi book 1, I am impressed with how hard I tried to study it. Maybe that's because I found something spiritual in it. My head was not comprehending it as much but my soul was attracted to it like a magnet. That's why I stuck with it. In the past, I sometimes wanted to stay away from the Faith but I couldn't because I knew that I would only fall apart if I did. In fact, there were always Bahá'í friends to help and encourage me. Through all these difficulties I came to understand that the Bahá'í Faith is like a guidepost and support for my life.

When I returned from Maxwell School in Canada I brought back a lot with me. But when I began to think about my immediate future plans, I couldn't think of anything. I was very nervous about the idea of not going to school or work. In Japan one is always made to think about the next plans for school or for work when one graduates from school. That is the norm. So at first it never occurred to me that I might spend time doing service or thinking about myself and my future. But, in the end, I decided to stay with or near my family for the time being so that I could think about what I should do for the next year and how I should live my life as a Bahá'í.

This decision was a determining factor for my future. If I were not a Bahá'í or if I had not gone to Maxwell School, I would not have made such a decision. What I am doing now is not a youth year of service in the strict sense. But I am spending my time studying certain things that I find useful and at the same time I help out with Bahá'í children's classes, Ruhi study circles and the like wherever I can be of some use. As I spend my time exploring various possibilities in my life, I have begun to see my future more clearly. I have thought about a lot of things: why I am living this life now, what I want to do, human relationships, my future. I sometimes got lost because there were so many questions. But it was the Bahá'í writings and Ruhi study circles that gave me the answers. When I let the Faith into my daily life, my life was enriched and spiritualized and my horizon expanded. The purpose of life is to know and love God. When we work on this goal, we gain a lot of 'treasures' for ourselves. In the past I tended to be carried away by the material forces around me but I have begun to have my own firm beliefs to protect me. My friends often ask me, 'So, what are you doing these days?' I answer that I am studying such and such and also teaching virtues to children. But my friends do not show much interest, saying 'What is that? So, what are you doing exactly?' I know it is partly because I have not been able to explain it effectively. So I am working on myself, polishing my heart and soul each day so that I will be able to teach the Faith better. I wish a bright future for the world.

Kurt Kreuger

Kurt Kreuger lives in Saskatoon, Saskatchewan and is taking an Engineering Physics degree at the University of Saskatchewan. He loves to travel and sees himself teaching after his education is complete. After writing this, he spent some time doing service at the Lotus Temple in India.

I am 23, I am taking Engineering Physics and have been a Bahá'í for almost a year. I was raised in the Lutheran church. My parents made me go until I was confirmed and then I was able to decide for myself. I stopped going to church because what was taught there didn't really interest me or answer my questions.

I didn't really start to question the religious stuff until I was about 20. Until then it was mostly philosophy and other 'non-God' things. I had always believed in a Creator, something greater than me, but I didn't know what. When I finally started asking questions about God, I kinda got into Buddhism and attended several services at a local temple. I began to read a little about Hinduism, Islam and other spiritual paths. The first person to introduce me to the Faith was in one of my physics classes at school. We met waiting around the physics building. After the first few 'What are you taking?'s and 'Where are you from?'s, the conversation veered towards world health. I had always been a thinker/philosopher and I had my own personal views on the problems afflicting mankind. It seemed to me that it was a lack of mutual respect. When I said that, my new friend said, 'Have you ever heard of the Bahá'í Faith? It's the newest world religion.' I was like, 'No. A world religion that I haven't heard of? Cool.' The bell rang then to end the discussion but much more was to be discussed in the near future.

I began a book 1 Ruhi course with several Bahá'ís, including this person, and regularly attended firesides. I also attended a conference sponsored by the Association for Bahá'í Studies. At first I was only interested in learning about the Faith and getting to know these people better. The main ideas of the Faith (i.e. the three onenesses) made so much sense. My father is very much an intellectual and I am much like him. He had many reservations about organized religion, so I did too. It wasn't until about a year after I had heard of the Faith that I started to seriously consider it for myself. There were several things that were difficult for me to accept, namely, the Bahá'í stance on homosexuality and alcohol, men only on the Universal House of Justice and the degree of chastity required of youth. The two things that let me get past all these obstacles were research and prayer. The more I researched and asked God if this was the truth, the more my mind opened to the truth of this Revelation. Finally, a year and a half after the Faith was introduced to me, I decided to accept it.

One of the strengths the Faith gives me is knowledge of a way to fix the problems we see in society. We all know stuff needs fixing but nobody knows how to do it. It also gives me a positive outlook for the future and the confidence to proceed with what I think will most benefit humanity.

Harsh Pancholi

Harsh Pancholi was raised mostly in Dubai, United Arab Emirates, and currently resides in Victoria, Canada. He is seeking a career in international development, so by the time you read this, he could be anywhere in the world!

I just finished my degree in anthropology from the University of Victoria after slogging it out for two and a half years straight. Right now I am in transition mode. It's the first time in my life I feel I have extricated myself from society's imposed institutional systems and it is quite a liberating feeling. I've thoroughly enjoyed my academic experience, despite it being extremely rigorous and all-consuming. It is a human trait to compartmentalize different aspects of one's life and keep them separate for various reasons. Maybe life is easier to manage that way. My academic experience is not removed from my growth as a spiritual, intellectual and moral human being. Everything in my life is centred around my Faith and I wouldn't have it any other way. In order to understand why I am a Bahá'í, it is necessary to journey back in time and document various processes and moments of my life.

I was born in Ahmedabad, India, which is just a few hours' train ride northwest of Bombay. My parents are both Indian and we've made our home in Dubai, U.A.E. for the past three decades. I spent my childhood in Dubai, my adolescence in India and my young adulthood in Canada. I grew up in a Hindu family and that was my religion by birth. Relatively speaking, we were a moderately religious family, with my grandmother spearheading all religious activities in the family. I was expected to be a Hindu all my life and follow in the footsteps of everyone else. This is not to say that my experience is in any way better than anyone else in my family because I chose the Bahá'í Faith over Hinduism but my journey is definitely not the same. The following account is my personal spiritual journey and feelings. It is in no way, shape or form a critique of Hinduism. I am just explaining how it was for me growing up as a Hindu.

Curiosity. This is a well that is exclusively the domain of children and it is always brimming with pails of questions. I was an extremely curious and inquisitive child and I've always strived to maintain that quality even now. There is still so much wonder in this world and I don't want to cease to be amazed. As a child I was the one with a million questions. People thought I was very cute because I had an overactive mind and imagination but I was truly trying to solve the mysteries of life by the time I was eight years old. Most of my inquiries were about 'religion' and 'God'. I wasn't satisfied with the status quo of Hinduism and the idea that you just believe because your forefathers and your family believe. I wanted concrete answers. Sometimes I wanted empirical answers as well. My constant interrogation didn't sit well with some of the adults and they told me that I shouldn't question religion because it is something that has been part of our culture for many millennia. There was also a misunderstanding between me and the adults. My questions were posed so that I could obtain a better understanding of the nature of religion and God. They took it that I was questioning the validity of their beliefs. As a child in a Hindu culture, you just don't do that. You don't question adults. You just show respect and accept anything they say to you as the truth. I never accepted that because I believed that adults weren't without error. I was known as the 'troublemaker' and the obnoxious kid who wouldn't take any answer at face value.

A WARM PLACE IN MY HEART

After my failed attempts to get any satisfactory answers from my family or family friends, I decided to go to the actual source. My grandmother frequented this particular temple near our house. It is a beautiful temple right in the middle of urban chaos but hidden away on a small hill. One could easily miss it driving by. It is about three kilometres away from our house and we used to walk there. One minute you're surrounded by two-way traffic and the next minute you're walking up this rugged path with birds chirping from trees. It is quite surreal. I decided to join my grandmother on her walks to the temple and put my questions to the priests. They would definitely have more insight than my family because they had studied the religion and were living a religious monastic life. To my surprise, they were baffled by my questions and they didn't have any new gems of wisdom to share with me. I would ask them, 'Why is it better to pray at a temple than in my room if my motivation for praying is the same?' 'Why are there so many gods and not just one God?' 'How do I know that God does exist?' 'Why do I have to follow these traditions and rituals?' All my questions were met with disgust and condescending answers. I was denigrated because I was a child and I couldn't possibly understand the intricacies of religion and its importance in one's life. This really bothered me because I wasn't taken seriously and it frustrated me because I wasn't getting any answers to my questions. After a few humiliating trips to the temple, I decided that I was never going to visit a temple again and I gave up my identity as a Hindu because I felt completely disconnected from the religion. I became an atheist and directed all my anger and frustration towards ultra-religious people in my community.

I decided that God didn't exist because if religion was from God and God is pure, then surely perversion of religion wouldn't occur. It would only occur because people made up all these fanciful stories and it was turned into this huge commercial enterprise. Everyone bought into this huge lie and now it was too late to turn back because it would destroy the very fabric of society. It is also very difficult not to pay attention to inequalities and hardships of life living in a country like India. If God loved everyone equally, then why was there so much pain and suffering? If God was all-powerful and mighty, He would right the wrongs. How could there be a God who was loving and indifferent to the conditions of mankind at the same time? I just couldn't wrap my head around these conundrums and came to the conclusion that God was just a conceptual tool that people used as a crutch to find some meaning in life. I thought I was so smart because I figured this out when I was around ten years old and I became determined not to let my life be governed by obsolete rules and useless traditions. As much as I tried to push away my curiosity and questions and take the intellectual route, though, somewhere in my being I was still longing to find God.

Fast forward to when I was 13 years old. I took a trip to New Delhi with my family to attend a wedding. After the wedding we had a couple of days to travel around town and visit some landmarks. One of them was the Lotus temple. I was excited about seeing everything else but that temple. I was whining and arguing all the way there. For me, there was no point because I'd been to scores of temples and they were the same and empty of any spirituality. We could've used that time to visit an archaeological site but my grandmother was adamant about going to the temple and there was no further discussion. They dragged me to the temple and I was in the most bitter mood because just that one act would undermine my analysis of God and religion.

I remember this day like it was yesterday. It is one of the most vivid and ethereal religious experiences of my life. I was transfixed by the sheer architecture of the temple and I stood outside for a long time, completely overwhelmed by this feeling of being so little. I walked in and to my utter surprise, there were no idols or pictures or statues to worship. People were sitting on benches and praying. I looked up and there was something written in Arabic, I deduced. People were praying and some were talking and all of this noise was filtered out. I was in my own bubble. For the first time in my life I wasn't sure what to do in a temple. I just sat down on a bench and watched other people. I was so completely taken aback that it didn't even register to me that I should ask someone about the temple's religious affiliation. I don't even remember how long I was in the temple or any other activities that we did that day. All

I can remember is just this one experience and how it completely reawakened something in me that was lying dormant. It would be years before I came to know that this was a Bahá'í temple.

After that, I wasn't really an atheist or a religious believer. I was somewhere in between. I knew in my heart that the answers were out there, I just had to be patient and make sure that I never gave up my search. Life has an interesting way of making things difficult and complicated. I was completely consumed by academics, sports and social activities and my search took a back seat. I would still think about it but I never had time to actively search for answers. In early 1997 a Muslim friend of mine became a Bahá'í. She gave me *The Seven Valleys and the Four Valleys* to read because she knew that it was probably the best book to introduce me to the Bahá'í Faith. It was the busiest time of my life and so I didn't really get around to reading it thoroughly. I was finishing my provincials and moving to Canada for further education. I remember making a mental note to get hold of that book again and give it due attention.

Things happened in fast forward that year and, before I knew it, I was in Canada, ready for a new adventure. We moved to Vancouver and my mom wanted us to go to a school there. After attending a public school in North Vancouver, we decided that it was better for us to go to a private school. Some friends told us that Vancouver Island had really good private schools and they gave us a directory of different ones. My mom called up various schools and one of them was Maxwell International Bahá'í School. Through sheer luck and circumstance, we ended up visiting Maxwell's campus before other private schools in the Shawnigan Lake area. We fell in love with the campus and the location and decided not to look any further. We went to the admission office and we literally got admitted to the school in 15 minutes. We had to catch the last ferry back to Vancouver and so everything happened at lightning speed. In hindsight, if we had looked at any other private school before Maxwell, we would never have attended it, not because the school isn't academically competent but other schools have better sports facilities. This reminds me of what my mom always says, 'Things always happen for a reason.'

I was thrust into a situation where I was constantly surrounded by Baháʼís and religious literature. At this point I was aware of the existence of the Baháʼí Faith and I was slowly investigating it. I was in an environment where I could safely explore the Faith and I cultivated friendships with people who were kind and eager to answer my questions. Six months into it, I knew that I had finally found what I had always been looking for. I did have many doubts and questions but I knew that I had to personally investigate the Faith and come to conclusions and realizations based on deep introspection. I wanted to become a Baháʼí but there were a few hurdles before that and I had to reconcile them. I didn't understand the need to sign a card to register as a member of a religion.[1] I just wanted to say that I was a Baháʼí and leave it at that. After countless months of agonizing over this, the answer came to me as an epiphany. I was just trying to find some reason not to accept the truth in my heart and I picked a really petty administrative aspect to have issues with. It is just a card and signing or not signing, it doesn't change how God is going to see me as a person. So instead of not signing it and trying to be a philosophical rebel, I knew that I should just sign it and get it over with. I also realized that, at the root of it, this was an issue of identity. If I didn't sign the card, then I could get away with some indiscretions and I could sit on the spiritual fence. Either you do it or you don't. I didn't want to be fluid in my religious identity depending on life circumstances. I realized that instead of me moulding my religion to my life, I had to mould my life to my religion and faith. I was walking around the University of Waterloo campus when this epiphany hit me. I stopped in my tracks, postponed whatever it was that I was going to do, walked towards the store of this Baháʼí gentleman I knew and signed my card right then and there. I also knew that I wasn't going to declare my faith at Maxwell because I wasn't comfortable with the open process. When someone signs the card and declares, it is announced at the next school assembly and people congratulate that person and welcome them into the Faith. Some

---

[1] Compiler's note: In many countries, a 'declaration card' is used when a person wishes to declare his or her faith. It is used as a simple administrative form to register the person as a Baháʼí, so that he or she can attend feasts, give to the Baháʼí fund and vote in Baháʼí elections, all of which only registered Baháʼís can do.

people need such affirmation and acceptance but for me this was much more personal. I wasn't comfortable with people applauding my decision and I didn't need any welcoming. My peers had only a small glimpse of my journey and I didn't feel that it was something to congratulate. The applauding is also done out of joy and happiness but I wanted to keep my personal growth a private process. I didn't become a Bahá'í just because of those two years at Maxwell. I've been on that journey since I was a young child and that journey is still going on. My declaration didn't culminate my spiritual journey, it just guided me in the right way.

My faith in God isn't something that was taught to me. My faith is something I actively worked towards and found through extreme hardship. I am a Bahá'í because I finally found the truth that was already embedded in me. I just had to discover it. I wrestled with many demons before I declared myself to be a Bahá'í. I had the bounty of meeting wonderful and understanding people who helped me in my spiritual quest. There are so many people I could name but the list would be way too long and I am not sure if they will accept any credit for my spiritual growth. It would also be incorrect to believe that my spiritual journey was solidified after I declared. I've had to deal with many tests and difficulties and there were times when I wanted to recant the Faith.

After Maxwell I expected Bahá'í communities to be homogenous in their spiritual attitude towards new Bahá'ís or seekers and I faced many tests living in different communities. One particular instance really put me off the Faith and I looked into what needed to be done to recant the Bahá'í Faith. After I found out that in order to recant I had to declare that I didn't believe the Bahá'í Prophets to be Manifestations of God, I realized that that was something I wasn't prepared to do. It also made me realize that my issues were somewhat petty in nature and to discard the Faith just because of that would be unjustifiable. If someone is actively going to pursue the path of finding faults within the Faith, they will find them. Upon closer inspection, one will realize that these faults aren't because there is a fallacy in the religion but are the result of imperfect human beings. The Guardian of the Bahá'í Faith has said that one of the biggest challenges faced by Bahá'ís will be other Bahá'ís. It was one of the most important lessons I learned as a new Bahá'í.

This brings me full circle. My faith isn't separate from the rest of my life. I will never cease to be a Bahá'í in any aspect of my life. It is an all-encompassing facet of everything I do and will do in the future. I didn't choose to go into social sciences because I could serve the Faith better. I chose it because I am truly passionate about making the world a better place, for my generation and for my children and their children. I've been involved in social and environmental activism since I was very young. I have been a volunteer with the World Wide Fund for Nature ever since I can remember and have worked with different environmental organizations and taken various trips with them to different parts of Northern India. It took me a while to figure out what I wanted to pursue at university, and after a few failed attempts, I decided to finish my degree in anthropology, the best decision I've made in my life. Even though the last two years were intense, I thoroughly enjoyed most of my classes and for the first time I felt that I was learning something constructive. It also gave me insight into the field of 'development' and what has worked and what hasn't. Improving the lives of people all over the world would have been accomplished by now if the problems could have been solved through material means alone. The unification of the world and the alleviation of social ills will only be accomplished through a balance between spiritual and material means. The Bahá'í Faith has given me this added perspective and I can see this because of the failure of development projects one after another all over the globe. This aspect of my faith has taken it from being just a personal intellectual pursuit and brought in an outward perspective. The Bahá'í Faith ties in my personal spiritual goals, academic goals and familial goals in one coherent path and it has given me a fulfilling spiritual lifestyle.

One of the most beautiful aspects of the Bahá'í Faith is the importance of independent investigation of truth. I can only recount the processes that helped me in my spiritual path but I can't put my finger on exactly what made me a Bahá'í. It was a mix of many different factors. I devoured the Bahá'í writings and voraciously read anything and everything I could get my hands on. My connection to the Faith was a practical one in the beginning. I saw the wisdom in the writings and the intrinsic spiritual beauty embedded within the words. I came to love particular prayers and meditations. Most of my early Bahá'í years were spent in deep study and introspection and less activity within the community. I felt that I needed to learn and understand the writings adequately before I could go and proclaim my identity as a Bahá'í. But I've come to balance both now because it is just impossible for me not to be involved with other Bahá'ís and with various activities. The writings provide me a strong intellectual and practical connection to the Faith and the prayers provide me the emotional connection. I knew that I couldn't just have one or the other because it would only take me personally so far in the long run.

It has taken me a few years to be comfortable with my Bahá'í identity owing to various tests, difficulties and doubts. I know that I've come out as a stronger individual in the end and I will continue to progress in my faith through my work, family and meeting new people all over the world. I truly apologize if I have offended anyone by providing a critical analysis of Hinduism. It is an experience that belongs to me only and I do not wish to belittle anyone else's belief in Hinduism or any other religion. Thank you for reading my story and I wish you continuous grace of God in all your endeavours. I would like to leave you with one of my favourite quotations from the Bahá'í writings. It is from the second most holy book of the Bahá'í Faith, the Kitáb-i-Íqán (The Book of Certitude):

> No man shall attain the shores of the ocean of true understanding except he be detached from all that is in heaven and on earth. Sanctify your souls, O ye peoples of the world; that haply ye may attain that station which God hath destined for you and enter thus the tabernacle which, according to the dispensations of Providence, hath been raised in the firmament of the Bayán. (Bahá'u'lláh, *Kitáb-i-Íqán*, p. 3)

Alláh-u-Abhá.

A WARM PLACE IN MY HEART

Hayley Miloff

Hayley Miloff was born in Jakarta, Indonesia, and was 16 at the time of writing. She is the youngest in the family of Maury Miloff and Helen de Marsh. She has two older brothers. The family has travelled all over the world but now make their home, at least temporarily, in Western Quebec, where Hayley is finishing high school in 2007. One has to wonder what will be next for her!

We were visiting my brother Ali, who was teaching English in Japan and living in a tiny apartment in Mobara, an hour outside of Tokyo. It was a special time since we were together as a family for two whole weeks after months of separation. What a joy to finally be together and exploring such a fascinating new country! My brother Zach flew in from Montreal. Mom, Dad and I came from Dhaka, Bangladesh. My Mom had brought with us duffel bags full of sleeping bags and blankets and anything warm she could find in our home to the Japanese winter we were visiting. If you know Japan, you will know that there is very little central heating. It was cold! But we were fine under layers of coats with little propane heaters coughing out a bit of heat. Most of all we were all together.

The night of the Feast of Honour arrived and we set out by car to find the gathering in a neighbouring city where there was a small community. On the way we realized that this was the anniversary of my Dad's declaration in 1973. As we pondered the wonder of that, I considered in my heart the decision I had been weighing for what seemed like ages. This could be the moment. I had been a Bahá'í all my life, having been raised in a Bahá'í family. But my own declaration was very personal and very much my own. At the same time, to share that special day with my Dad was an opportunity not to be missed. On top of that, it was the six month anniversary of the passing of my dear grandfather. It was also nearly New Year's Eve and it marked the beginning of something new for me.

I took a deep breath and told the family crammed into the small car speeding towards the feast that I had an announcement to make. There was a hush and pause as everyone stopped and heard me. I stated that at that moment I was making my declaration of belief in Bahá'u'lláh. Joy and a moment in family history. Everything was peaceful and quiet. After that there was no need to talk. Later, Dad said that before I made my announcement he had had a sense of anticipation that something wonderful was about to happen. Naturally, when we arrived at the tiny feast gathering, there was great excitement. The next day at a Unity Feast to mark the New Year at the Tokyo Bahá'í Centre, a declaration card was produced and a friend translated it. I have the Japanese version framed on my wall. It doesn't have a word of English on it and that makes it even more special. I was a counted as a new Bahá'í in Japan, in Bangladesh and again in Canada when I returned last summer. I like to think I skewed the statistics just a little in the right direction!

Priscilla Fang

as told to Enoch Tanyi in Cameroon

Priscilla Fang is a 28-year-old seamstress in Cameroon who lost her shop in a fire that swept the market in which she operated. Soon after this reverse in life she underwent a surgical operation and the surgeon advised her not to use her legs to pedal the sewing machine. Obliged to earn a living, she took a job as a bartender – a job that requires her to work from 8 a.m. till midnight, and beyond on some occasions, and leaves her little time for rest. These adversities were paramount in her thoughts and a cause of constant worry to her. This is the story she told me.

On the 7th of March 2007 Priscilla was trying to get some sleep after a hard day's work when she had a mystic experience. A voice told her, 'Follow God and all your problems will be solved.' She woke up thinking, 'Oh, my God! Does it mean that all these years

I have not been worshipping you enough or in the right way?'

That morning one of her neighbours, Celine, came by and during their brief chat mentioned that she was going to see a certain Bahá'í lady. Priscilla had heard the name 'Bahá'í' before but had not taken any pains to enquire about it. But since this name came up again only hours after she had been told to follow God, implying that she possibly had not really been following God in her Roman Catholic worship, she started reflecting on the possible connection between that instruction and 'Bahá'í'. Then and there her desire to find out more about 'Bahá'í' was kindled.

At work that morning a bevy of chattering ladies ambled into the inn where Priscilla was working and took their seats in the garden. The International Women's Day celebration was over and the women had come in to socialize. They ordered some drinks. When Priscilla brought them to the table, she overheard part of a conversation between two ladies, one the same Celine who had come to her early in the morning and the other Emerencia.

Celine said to Emerencia, 'You've turned down the offer of a bottle of beer. Isn't it?'

'Yes, indeed', replied Emerencia.

'Is it because you are a Bahá'í?' asked Celine.

Emerencia nodded. 'Yes, indeed.'

The lady who had ordered the drinks turned to Priscilla, who was waiting to take the rest of the orders, and offered her a bottle of beer too.

'Thank you,' said Priscilla, 'but I don't drink beer.'

Priscilla was intrigued when she heard the word 'Bahá'í' again, especially as it was associated with the non-consumption of alcohol, a quality she loved and had developed. It was only because of her extreme need that she had to work in a place that sold alcohol because she could not find any other employment in Tiko.

She pressed the ladies to tell her more about the Bahá'í Faith and after a brief introduction was given, she concluded in her heart that the Bahá'í Faith must be the direction in which the voice she had heard at night was pointing. She then expressed her desire to become a Bahá'í.

A few days later she signed her declaration card and has since immersed herself in studying the Bahá'í teachings, devoting part of her quieter morning periods to that.

'I want to go deep into the Bahá'í Faith and one day go on pilgrimage,' she declared.

Priscilla is already facing stiff opposition from her employer, who does not approve of her leaving the Catholic church and has threatened her with dismissal if she continues to adhere to the Bahá'í Faith.

When I heard about Priscilla, I visited her at her workplace and gave her a gift of a prayer book. A few days later, as she sat reading the prayer book during a lull in business, her boss walked up to her, snatched the prayer book away and threw it outside. Priscilla quietly went and picked it up, taking her first lessons in suffering for the Faith.

Michael Skuce

My name is Michael Skuce. I became a Bahá'í in February 2006 at the age of 25, in Sooke, B.C. I am currently living in Ottawa, Ontario, and preparing to enter teacher's education.

In the short period of eight months that I have been a member of the Bahá'í Faith, I have been asked the question 'Why did you become a Bahá'í?' many times. In every instance I have offered an intellectual explanation, laying out the myriad reasons why the Faith of Bahá'u'lláh makes sense to me. I talk about progressive revelation, the social teachings and practices of the Faith and Bahá'u'lláh's teachings on spiritual reality. I explain that these concepts immediately resonated with me in a way that was so clear and coherent that I acknowledged within a very short period of time that I believed this to be the truth, that I was a Bahá'í. Using my rational mind, discovering the truth of Bahá'u'lláh's mission was like placing a square peg in a square hole.

What I don't really discuss with anybody is how becoming a Bahá'í was also very much an intuitive process. During my transition from seeker to Bahá'í there were moments when it became shockingly clear to me that I had been led to this spiritual renewal, this new life, this great honour by the hand of God. Brief flashes of insight came where all the events of the past five years, the period of time that I could really say I was a 'spiritual seeker', seemed to fit together perfectly, one by one leading me out of the dark forest of uncertainty to the ocean of certitude.

For me these are the sweetest, most awe-inspiring moments on the magical mystery tour of life. But they are also the moments I am least likely to mention when discussing my reasons for being a Bahá'í. Why? I feel that if I were to put forward these reasons I might sound 'wishy-washy'. Perhaps I just haven't yet met and had deep spiritual conversation with enough new Bahá'ís. Coming to the Faith from an entirely non-Bahá'í background, I am usually explaining this to someone who knows very little about the Faith, so it is also a teaching opportunity and I want to be as factual and informative as possible. Or, as has happened, I may be explaining this to someone close to me who is quite sceptical about my new journey. Certainly in this situation I want to get across, as concisely as I can, the practical reasons first.

Far from being wishy-washy or anti-intellectual, these glimpses of divine guidance and confirmations are the sources of certitude which inspire and guide my intellectual pursuit and discovery of Bahá'u'lláh's teachings. I just tend to keep them to myself right now. Maybe I just like it that way; it's kind of like not kissing-and-telling.

Dona Séléger

Introduction and translation by Julie Benoit Séléger

Dona Séléger was born in 1976 and grew up in a small town in the south of Haiti. At 14 he moved to Port-au-Prince to pursue his education and subsequently discovered the Bahá'í Faith. He went on to graduate from the Université d'État d'Haiti with a degree in Public Administration. Dona (known to his friends and family as Fanfan) now lives in Ottawa and is just finishing up a second university degree, this one in International Management from the University of Ottawa. He loves making and listening to music, playing and watching soccer, buying and reading books and spending time with loved ones, including his wife Julie Benoit Séléger, a Canadian whom he met when she was doing Bahá'í service in Haiti.

I first came into contact with the Bahá'í community when I was 13 years old because my oldest brother was already a Bahá'í and he used to bring books and pamphlets to the house. At that time, I still lived in my hometown of Jérémie, located in the south of Haiti. I also knew an American Bahá'í pioneer named Glen Bouchard because my brother worked for him and when I visited his house he always invited me to read Bahá'í books and writings. In 1991 there was a *coup d'état* in my country and, because we were in the middle of a political crisis, all the public schools were closed. Both my parents had recently passed away very suddenly and I had no choice but to move to the capital, Port-au-Prince, to live with my aunts.

When I arrived in the capital I got back into contact with Glen Bouchard, who now lived there as well, and he asked me to help out with a translation project that he had undertaken for the Bahá'í community. The project consisted of translating Bahá'í writings from French into Haitian Creole because the majority of Haitians don't understand French.

I agreed to help out and that's how I came into direct contact with the Bahá'í writings without having someone actually 'teach' me the Faith. I remember the first book that we started to translate. It was a speech that 'Abdu'l-Bahá had given in New York in 1912. The words were so touching, so beautiful; they attracted me like a magnet.

At that point I started to participate in all the activities of the Bahá'í community, like youth classes and a Dance Workshop, as well as deepening groups every Sunday at the National Bahá'í Centre of Haiti. I must say, after the writings themselves, the next thing that touched me profoundly was the hospitality I received from the Bahá'í community. At a certain point it became difficult for me to tell the difference between the family relationships I had with my siblings, my aunts and my cousins and the family relationship I was establishing in the Bahá'í community. With the Bahá'ís I felt like I was at home. At the age of 15 I decided to become a Bahá'í. Incredibly enough, all this love I felt from the Bahá'í writings and from the community helped me to move past the trials I had faced surrounding my parents' deaths. The Bahá'í Faith became my surrogate family.

Eric Michell

Eric Michell was 27 years old at the time of writing and living in Montreal. He has three half brothers whom he considers brothers and loves dearly. He studied environmental sciences at the University of Waterloo and plans on returning for a Master's degree. He is interested in learning and teaching anything there is to find out about life – biology, chemistry, history, mathematics, human relationships. He loves reading about nature, the environment and sciences and enjoys helping others.

I was born in Montreal in the summer of 1978. My parents are from different linguistic backgrounds: my mother is a French Canadian from Quebec and my father is English Canadian from Ontario. My parents met when they were Bahá'ís back in the late 1970s. They got married but separated when I was two years old. I have lived since then with two different families. I lived with my mother until I was ten years old. Then when I was 11 my father decided that I should live with him and eventually with my stepmother, when they got married. At 16 I left Montreal for Ottawa to live with my father's brother for two years, then went to Waterloo to study environmental sciences at the University of Waterloo for five years. I then returned to Montreal.

My father has been a Bahá'í for the past 30 years or so but my mother decided to change religions around the time my parents divorced. My father talked to me on occasions about the Bahá'í Faith and its principles and I went to Bahá'í feasts as a young child but he never really taught me the Faith. What really changed for me was when I met a Bahá'í girl when I was 16 years old. She showed so much love and caring for everyone around her that she really started to inspire me about the Bahá'í Faith. I kept in contact with her through all of those years but never really investigated the Faith seriously until the summer of 2002, the year I returned to Montreal from attending the University of Waterloo.

I declared as a Bahá'í in September 2002, partly because of meeting a girl but also because I believe very much in the principles of the Bahá'í Faith and decided to immerse myself in the teachings. I didn't know at the time what it meant to become a Bahá'í and what would be required of me as a Bahá'í, but I will always remember when I signed my card in front of a member of the Local Spiritual Assembly. He asked me 'Do you know what you are getting yourself into?' I told him, 'No, but I have the feeling that I am soon going to find out.' We both laughed. What struck me most was the joy, companionship and love that can be felt in people. At that point I didn't know how to immerse myself in the teachings in terms of obligatory prayers, fasting and so on. For the first year or so I wasn't very involved in the community besides attending some feasts.

In May of 2003 I met a Bahá'í who asked my father if he knew anyone who would be interested in organizing a conference commemorating the United Nations International Day of the Environment. I was told of this opportunity and I thought that it would be nice to start being more involved in the community. I had such a good time organizing and hosting the conference that eventually we decided with the other Bahá'ís in the community to start a Bahá'í study circle on the environment to promote environmental thinking in the community.

In September 2003 I started studying Ruhi book 1, *Reflections on the Life of the Spirit*. It was the first time that I had had an opportunity to learn more about the life of the soul from a Bahá'í perspective. I met many wonderful people doing the book, one of whom I became interested in. We started getting to know each other better but then my past crept up on me. Nothing happened of that friendship and I realized at that time that I had much pain and anger inside of me that was keeping me from growing up and being active in the community. That was the turning point for me in my life.

The teachings and prayers of the Faith, with the moral support of my father, helped me deal with all of the emotions that had been buried inside me for many years. Little by little, I read more and more of the teachings, such as the Kitáb-i-Aqdas, prayed every day, went to more and more Bahá'í events such as 19 Day Feasts and, more importantly, started looking at a new model to follow in my life. That model was 'Abdu'l-Bahá and the writings of Bahá'u'lláh.

At that point in my life I felt that if I wanted to change something in a positive way in society, education, and especially children's education, would be the most effective way since children are looking for models to follow. I was given the opportunity to teach children two years after declaring. I felt ready to devote myself to the Bahá'í Faith as an active member of the community. At first I wasn't sure how I could help the community but with time I discovered my strengths and was given different opportunities to serve. I also discovered a book written by a Bahá'í, for educators, about how to teach the virtues to children and how to teach them in a respectful manner. It also called upon me to become more virtuous myself.

What I read in an article published by the Association of Bahá'í Studies also enlightened me. It talked about following the Bahá'í principles because Bahá'u'lláh said to do so in His writings. I realized that when you follow the writings with no investigation, in any religion for that matter, you are blinded by them. I decided to investigate and follow some of the writings even though they were contrary to what I believed in at the time. After following the teachings with critical thinking, I discovered to my astonishment why those writings were given to us. I saw the positive effects they had on me. It was also a time when I decided to fast according to the letter. It was absolutely an amazing experience. No words can possibly describe such a feeling but the sacrifice of food for the nourishment of the soul has had a spiritually uplifting effect on me.

One thing that I realized through this experience is that we must drink from the cup of truth, which Bahá'u'lláh has so graciously and lovingly given to us, and more importantly, to share those words with others around us, so they may also fall in love with Bahá'u'lláh.

The more I study and meditate on the teachings of Bahá'u'lláh, 'Abdu'l-Bahá and Shoghi Effendi, the better understanding I have of the purpose of the Bahá'í Faith in this world and the more love I have for others around me, especially my parents.

Ilya Shodjaee-Zrudlo

Ilya Shodjaee-Zrudlo completed the liberal arts programme at CEGEP Heritage College in Quebec. He lives in Chelsea, Quebec, with his family and planned to go to university immediately but ended up taking a year off to do service at the Bahá'í World Centre in Haifa, Israel, commencing in autumn 2006. Ilya grew up in a Bahá'í family. He loves to play jazz/blues piano, read, watch movies, listen to his music and be completely ridiculous.

My name is Ilya. I am an extroverted 17 year old. I am a Bahá'í.

I grew up in a Bahá'í family, so naturally, I thought, what else could I be other than a Bahá'í? I signed a card declaring my faith on my fifteenth birthday and that was that. I had been to children's classes most of my childhood and I am a Ruhi tutor. Until a few months ago, though, my life had little direction and the only focus the Bahá'í Faith had in my life was occasional teaching, Bahá'í camps and hanging out with Bahá'í youth.

Recently, I have become enthralled with my programme at school. I'm in a liberal arts programme at CEGEP in Quebec, Canada, and it is one of the greatest things that ever happened to me. My courses, teachers and environment completely changed.

CEGEP is entirely different from high school as the people who are there (for the most part) *want* to learn, are interested and have open minds. I had lots of opportunities to teach and I eventually realized that although I knew a lot about Bahá'í administration, the covenant, the history and basic concepts, I wasn't actually very good at transmitting the essence of the Bahá'í Faith and its teachings to people. I realized my incompetence fully when encountering very specific questions from my religion teacher. Although he was satisfied with my answers and wants me to take an hour of his class next semester and talk about the Bahá'í Faith, I never felt that I answered his questions well enough. I always felt that there was something I should be saying that would 'blow his socks off'. Progressive revelation and independent investigation of the truth has kept his curious mind satisfied for now but I think he wants to know more. I lent him a book; I will lend him another. Between my teacher's questions, the growing interest I had in philosophy, religion and learning and my increasingly critical mind, I had a growing excitement about life and the day I live in.

One day my father asked me if I had read the *Tablets of Bahá'u'lláh*, and I replied that I hadn't. He went through a list and I realized that I had not read *any* source texts of the Bahá'í Faith. This strongly discouraged me and I set myself to begin reading *Gleanings from the Writings of Bahá'u'lláh* and then *Some Answered Questions* by 'Abdu'l-Bahá. Through reading these texts, and listening in all my classes, I saw little connections beginning to establish themselves between any great art, literature, poetry, movement, great philosophers and writers and the Bahá'í Faith. The Bahá'í Faith seems to encompass everything. It is more than a belief-system or a few laws; it contains, in all the hundreds of volumes of knowledge, all the truths and mysteries of the physical and spiritual world. Now I have a new philosophical and academic focus on the Bahá'í Faith, which makes me comfortable teaching it and influences me greatly in the paths that I choose.

A few things Bahá'ís have told me, or I have read, have greatly changed the way I think and have stuck with me permanently. Here are a few of the striking ideas that have stuck with me.

Recently I have been able to sit with any one of my friends and, if I really concentrate on the person, I can see why he or she is my friend. I can see his or her good qualities and only that. If I focus on those, I tend to enjoy everybody's company, even if I somewhat disliked that person before.

I heard somewhere an interesting talk about Bahá'í identity. It somewhat refocused the way I think about being a Bahá'í. Being a Bahá'í really imbues your whole life. The Bahá'í Faith is not a religion as we define them and see them today; it is a whole different life, a life of service. I have come to realize that my life is defined by the Bahá'í Faith and not any other way. The Bahá'í Faith is intrinsically linked to my own person: 'My name is Ilya and I *am* a Bahá'í.' I am a Bahá'í all the time, every second that I breathe and every decision I make reflects my Bahá'í identity. I am not only a Bahá'í when I feel like it, or on Sundays, or when my parents tell me to be.

I talked to a friend of mine at length about her point of view on the Bahá'í Faith and certain components of it, like teaching and declaration. She really emphasized listening and from then on I have always tried to listen a little more than I used to. Listening to someone else's point of view instead of forcing your own upon them or trying to argue with them about it does not work. Even if the other person is promoting the most outrageous point of view you have ever heard, it is always better to listen first and get them to talk. Reconciliation between two points of view is almost always possible since nothing is white and black. Unity in diversity is such a fundamental principle in the Bahá'í Faith! Diversity is *fundamental* to unity: there could be no unity without diversity of races, language, culture *and opinions*. If we all thought the same there would be no need for a religion at all. Unity is impossible without plurality. People will always think different things and have various opinions on issues. This diversity should be a source of growth and learning. Listening to someone else's point of view can *never* hurt. I try to listen more nowadays and I think it has paid off.

This thought actually came to me from the movie *Groundhog Day* but it runs parallel to Bahá'í teachings. Putting meaning into your actions in life makes everything so much more worthwhile. If you actually try and learn things from people and try to grasp something from the wealth of knowledge that is constantly flowing around you, your life will have *meaning*. If you take time to practise skills or learn an instrument or build relationships and make new friends, your life becomes rich. I have taken the effort to actually do meaningful things with people and every few days I feel better and more accomplished.

Finally, the idea of a year of service has got me very excited. I have not gone on one yet but from what I have heard, I need to go on a year of service soon! The idea of serving in Haifa, being around all these young people and all these incredibly intelligent minds and servants of the Faith, participating in workshops every night of the week in Israel with the other pioneers and youth . . . a year there would completely change me and perhaps let me know what I want to do in life!

I am a Bahá'í because of my parents, because of my Bahá'í friends, because of Bahá'í youth, because of extraordinary members of the Bahá'í Faith, because of experience in the world with a Bahá'í background and because of the will I have to spread the word of God and to have a very good time in doing so. Telling people about the Bahá'í Faith, learning and being with my friends are the three greatest things in my life right now and in the near future I might add 'years of service', although one of those might consist of a composition of the three aforementioned elements of my life.

I have always wondered what it would be like if I had not grown up in a Bahá'í family but had learnt about the Bahá'í Faith from a friend. Would I have become a Bahá'í? Would I have been me? But who am I, really? I am a Bahá'í.

Kira Baskerville

Kira Baskerville lives in Canada. Formerly home-schooled, she now attends high school.

I am Kira Baskerville. I'm 13 and live in Quebec, Canada. I've been a Bahá'í since I was four, when my mother became a Bahá'í. Last year, my sister, Heather, chose to remain a Bahá'í when she turned 15. And my dad joined the Bahá'í Faith in June 2005, partly as a result of our family's pilgrimage in early 2005, so the members of my whole immediate family are Bahá'ís now.

Why have I chosen to become a Bahá'í? Originally, because my mom became a Bahá'í, my sister and I did also. After a year or so of being a very young Bahá'í, I began to understand the significance of being a Bahá'í. Without religion, life isn't as meaningful and you don't know what your purpose is. You can feel desperate.

I was, luckily, brought into this Faith by my mom. To me, I am a Bahá'í because it feels right. What does that mean? Well, you are brought into a religion and find out it's the one for today. You learn what progressive revelation means. It's new, our religion. The other religions have changed over time but today is the day for the Bahá'í Faith. This day is like when a magazine issue is current. Each religion has its time to shine but then that time passes and then we find it's time for a new issue. It's exactly like that.

The Faith drew my heart. At first the feasts seemed a little boring but that's before I was involved and could understand well and could read.

From the very beginning, though, I felt all that love in the room and everyone's happiness. I enjoyed the treats as well! Around Bahá'ís I have always felt comfortable. They're like my family and I don't have to worry about doing something weird and being criticized or picked on for doing it.

In this culture there is alcohol. I don't feel comfortable around people when they are drinking. At Bahá'í gatherings you never have to worry about that. These are some of the reasons I am a Bahá'í.

A WARM PLACE IN MY HEART

Natasha Sinniece Collishaw

Natasha is a sixth generation Bahá'í and the granddaughter of a very exuberant woman, Acqdas Javid, who has served Dundas, Ontario with firesides for over 40 years. Her mother, Ladan Javid, is a gifted visual artist and vice-president of a solar energy company. Her father, Jim Collishaw, enjoys farming. She has three gorgeous sisters, Nassim, Anissa and Skye. Natasha, born in Thornhill, Ontario, beside the National Bahá'í Centre of Canada, has lived in many parts of the world – Ontario, Prince Edward Island, Fiji, as well as Ecuador and French Guyana where she had the bounty of serving as a pioneer. She currently lives in Ottawa, Ontario where she is in the School of Journalism and International Relations at Carleton University.

Why I Try to be Bahá'í

I try to be Bahá'í because I smell the injustice in the world.
The reek of our children's rotting corpses assaults my nose
As rich babies' balloon bellies induce repose
When there is enough food to feed them all three times
If not for the fragrance coming from Haifa's rose
The stench is so sickening I would hurl

I want a world where I can smell more hyacinths than beer
Where people are not derided for smelling of sumptuous curry
Where inhaling nicotine does not drive a mother into fury
And force her to leave with her arm over the baby's mouth in a hurry
I want a world where smelling your city's air is not a worry
Today in a part of Haifa Israel you can smell and breathe freer

I try to be Bahá'í because I taste stale solutions to troubles of the human race
Just as McDonald's french fries are the body's curse
Plastic, textureless, flavourless driving you straight to the hearse
Religious leaders are in centuries-old hatred immersed
Inciting their diminishing congregations to ignore all sacred verse
In order to fill up an obese, still-expanding, coin-jingling purse

Away from God, religion, truth and honour, they are turning their face

The Columbian Bahá'ís are offering a mint-fresh solution
That is now the property of the world as a whole
Fusing science and religion and other opposite poles
Bringing in some cases hip-hop, sign language, sponge painting and rock and roll
Helping all people begin to understand the nature of their soul
The constant exposure to the creative world cleaning out the thought pollution

I try to be Bahá'í because I feel a cold, crisp dollar bill in every greeting
And many of my human interactions are really that thin
Because in every conversation people are looking to win
Power, money, or beauty for themselves or their kin
And I find myself trapped in this same legitimization of sin
Unless I strive every day to bring celestial thoughts to every meeting

What we need is to love every part of God's creation
As if it were our sister, our father, our cousin, our aunt or our son
When a beautiful girl walking in darkness is greeted by 'hey hun'
Realistically dark visions would not fill her mind, nor would she run
Because she lives in a world where selfishness and hatred is just about done
A world where security is not thought of in terms of only the nation

I try to be Bahá'í because I hear the clamorous shouts and cries
Of a divided, crumbling, polarized society
Where there is no semblance of piety
Where people worship their culture as deity
And see 'the others' as something to despise
By loving the world you love your culture more, say Bahá'ís

And I have heard this in the dense forests of French Guyana
Where the 'boom boom' of at least five different drums starts
And the rhythms begin to divide up into at least ten different parts
And people that by day peddle down the street with their fruit carts
Create a sound and an energy that transforms and elevates all hearts
As I praise Bahá'u'lláh in a language I don't understand, I feel nirvana

I am a Bahá'í because I see an old world falling apart and a new one building up
Before my eyes when Bahá'u'lláh allows me to see
When I surf the Internet, read magazines, newspapers, or watch TV
Glimmers of truth shine wedged between materialism and pornography
More children see the world as one sea, one tree, really one country
Bahá'u'lláh's Revelation can make this a breathing, dancing and singing reality

I know this because I have seen the transforming power of the word of God
I have studied how it turns backward societies into enlightenment
I see Bahá'u'lláh every day turn normal people into the heaven-sent
I have seen His prayers drain my heart's sorrow and fill it with contentment
I have seen His words lead families to consultation instead of argument
Whether in Fiji, French Guyana, Ecuador or Canada, this Faith is something to laud

A WARM PLACE IN MY HEART

Tahereh Haji

Tahereh Haji was born in 1986 in Edmonton, Alberta, Canada to parents of Iranian background. She and her family moved to Saskatoon, Saskatchewan, in 1991. Tahereh has two younger siblings, a brother Anis and a sister Farah. She is working on her undergraduate degree in Biochemistry. Serving the Bahá'í Faith is her main goal in life and she is blessed to have many opportunities to do so. Tahereh also loves to write (literature, not composition) and play music. In her spare time she reads or spends time with Farah, who is now (2006) just two and a half years old.

I've often wondered why I am a Bahá'í. I know that the idea is quite cheesy . . . but I don't know what I did to deserve this blessing. Yet it's the simple truth. Perhaps that feeling, in itself, is part of it.

My childhood was spent pioneering and watching my parents serve. They instilled in me a natural willingness to participate in community activities, or rather an inability to say 'no', take your pick! The net result, however, is that, from a young age, my Bahá'í friends and I were planning activities and doing what we could for the Cause. The earliest such enterprise began when I was nine years old. My best friend and I (she was but seven years old) initiated a 'Fund Club' – I remember we had binders and we typed up forms. We contacted all of our Bahá'í friends to ask them to join and started to have games at the 19 Day Feast celebrations. Our parents were quite reliable; we never missed a single feast. All of the proceeds would go directly to the Fund. At one point, perhaps when I was 11 or 12, the Local Spiritual Assembly of our locality asked us (my friend, my little brother and me) to give a presentation about the Fund. I'll never forget how much work went into those meagre five minutes! We didn't want to let the Spiritual Assembly down . . .

Well, I daresay that was the beginning. I have done many things since then and it is not my wish to make this a copy of my resumé. Yet the story serves to make a point. When I affirmed my faith in Bahá'u'lláh, at the age of 15, I remember my reasoning behind it. I had thought long and hard during the months approaching that day. You see, I am not a person who can feel something and act based on that feeling – I can certainly make a comeback that quickly to something that has been said but make a decision? No. That I cannot do. As such, my reasoning came down to a comparison of the Faith with other religions. I found I was also unable to change who I was. I realized that the Bahá'í Faith was such an integral part of my life that were I not to sign my Bahá'í declaration card, I would continue acting as if I had! I trusted in God that He would affirm me spiritually one day and I must say, He's done so in a funny way... As the Hand of the Cause of God William Sears wrote: *God loves laughter*!

Well, I cannot pinpoint a single event that has done the trick but only to a series of them. The details are unimportant; suffice it to say that I have discovered that my life is, much like anyone else's, a series of crises and victories. Each time I stray a little from the protection of the Faith, God reaches out and provides me with a new path of service. It began with a simple club and now it happens to me almost on a regular basis, to an almost creepy extent. This is how I find myself personally confirmed spiritually.

On a global scale I find that the Five Year Plan is just one gigantic confirmation! The transformation that I see in my own community and in other places in the world is amazing. And the term 'unity in diversity' really applies. To think that the entire planet is broken up into clusters, and in each of these clusters the friends and their friends are doing the four core activities (study circles, devotional gatherings, children's classes and junior youth programmes) is mind-boggling. I did a bit of travelling this summer and I had the opportunity to see how different places do the same things – and it is absolutely brilliant. The Plan also allows the friends to immediately have a path of service when they arrive in a new place. It has made the Bahá'í world into one small community. As Bahá'u'lláh says: 'The earth is but one country...' (Bahá'u'lláh, *Gleanings*, p. 250)

I guess that this is why I am a Bahá'í in 2005. I look around and I see how decrepit this old world order is. Then I look at the vision of the Bahá'í Faith (read the Peace Message... that really sums it all up), and I see what the world needs to be if it intends on surviving – and only faith can transform it. The Bahá'í Faith provides the answers for all three levels of society: the individual, the community and the institutions.

And so, why not?

In fact, one has no choice in the matter, really. Bahá'u'lláh says in the Tablet of Aḥmad that 'he who turns away from this Beauty hath also turned away from the Messengers of the past and showeth pride towards God from all eternity to all eternity'. I know that this is the Truth; therefore, I must act. I must be a Bahá'í.

Kai Bighorn

Hello, my name is Kai Bighorn. I am of Native descent. My cultural background is Sioux and Chickasaw.

I was born into a Bahá'í family, so that would make me second generation. When I was born, my dad still hadn't declared himself as a Bahá'í; he was still a practising Christian. So you can imagine how difficult it was for my mom, who wanted to educate me about the Bahá'í Faith, but she had to do it carefully so as not to upset my father. To make matters even more complicated, my father would take me to church on Sundays, which could be very confusing when you're already trying to be taught about a different religion. But that is the beauty of being a kid: you don't know how to react in those kinds of situations, your heart is still pure. You are more accepting; you don't know how to judge anything.

My dad declared himself to be a Bahá'í in 1985ish, to my mom's relief, and finally I could be brought up without a tug of war between the Christian and Bahá'í Faiths. If I could only write about the joy my mom felt. There really is no way to describe it! Just know there were many, many smiles!

I enjoyed going to children's classes immensely. To tell the truth, it was a pain to go at first but, believe me, you couldn't tear me away when I was there. My faith was tested, however, as when I was no more than eight years old, I was sexually abused by someone outside the family. We all know that God gives us tests that will try and perfect us; we should also know that He will not give us tests that we ourselves cannot overcome. We always find a lesson in every test we are given. 'Abdu'l-Bahá explains,

> The souls who bear the tests of God become the manifestations of great bounties: for the divine trials cause some souls to become entirely lifeless, while they cause the holy souls to ascend to the highest degree of love and solidity. ('Abdu'l-Bahá, quoted by the Universal House of Justice in a letter to an individual, 2 December 1985)

I know deep down in my heart that I was being looked after by all the manifestations of God during my trials. I failed in a sense when it came to who to blame. In the beginning I blamed myself because I was taught 'right touch, bad touch' from an early age but what was I supposed to do? I was eight and no one at any age should have to go through that. I then went against my Faith and blamed it for not being there for me. I feel I didn't learn from my test because the abuse happened a second time. This time it sent me down a spiral staircase of tests and difficulties that would not have happened had I realized that everything happens for a reason. Any kind of test that happens to you is for some divine reason.

At that stage I hated being a Bahá'í because I felt that I was let down. I rebelled by not saying my prayers, by smoking, by not being trustworthy. But you know, the funny thing is I still smiled and had my usual upbeat attitude during that time. I just didn't want to draw attention to myself because at that time I hadn't disclosed that I had been abused. The real thing that hurt me the most was when I tried committing suicide. I had reached the bottom of the pit and was hurting emotionally and spiritually. I wasn't praying at all and, looking back, those prayers would have helped a lot.

Now don't get me wrong, I really wanted to be Bahá'í, really I did, but I was so tired of everything, from running from my problems to living a lie. I went to the extreme of signing my declaration card at 15 but in my heart I didn't feel like a Bahá'í. It wasn't that I was not practising as a Bahá'í – I went to feasts and conferences. I knew if I didn't get out of this lifestyle it would kill me in the end. I finally told my parents about what had happened and that step was a lifesaver; to have that heavy load lifted off my shoulders was a Godsend. I started to read and study the Bahá'í writings more and attended more Bahá'í functions, this time with a healed heart that was ready to listen.

I had the bounty of joining Wildfire Dance Theatre for a year of service and, let me tell you, tests and difficulties were flying in my face at every angle. But now that I have accepted the Faith and the realization that tests and difficulties are essential to one's life, I think that year helped me grow into a much more grounded Bahá'í. The Bahá'í writings state:

> The more difficulties one sees in the world the more perfect one becomes. The more you plough and dig the ground the more fertile it becomes. The more you cut the branches of a tree the higher and stronger it grows. The more you put the gold in the fire, the purer it becomes. The more you sharpen the steel by grinding the better it cuts. Therefore, the more sorrows one sees the more perfect one becomes. That is why, in all times, the Prophets of God have had tribulations and difficulties to withstand. The more often the captain of a ship is in the tempest and difficult sailing the greater his knowledge becomes. Therefore I am happy that you have had great tribulations and difficulties . . . Strange it is that I love you and still I am happy that you have sorrows. ('Abdu'l-Bahá, quoted in *Star of the West*, vol. 14, no. 2, p. 41)

Also, as a Native American in this day and age, to mention that you are a Bahá'í is a big task. It is a bounty to be able to go into Native communities and spread the word of God. Most of you already know that there is a great distrust towards the white race in regard to the use of residential schools and the injustice towards our people throughout history. So for a Native to see one of their own on stage dancing, fighting issues like poverty, drug and alcohol abuse, gangs and racism, tells there is hope. It is unusual to see a Native on stage who doesn't drink or do drugs, but with that said, it tells them again there is hope. The problem I think with our Native youth today is that they are living proof of the cycle their parents lived when they were their children's age. Their parents went through the residential school system, which created a lot of anger, led to the bottle and cut their hopes and aspirations. So you can imagine the bounty I feel when I travel to remote communities and help with the healing process, which will hopefully lead to better lives.

So you can get from this message that service is a big part of my life. It has really helped me through a lot of things. It seems each time I do service, there is a BIG test and difficulty waiting for me. But every time I try and tell myself this is God's will and there is always a reason why I am being tested. In a prayer concerning service it is said:

> At this time, I beg Thee, oh My God, by the Light of Thine Eternity, whereby the heavens and earth are illumined, to make My Feet of iron by which I may stand in His service, and the service of whosoever loveth Thee, that I may become a helper of Thy Religion, and a guardian of Thine Orders, until I suffer martyrdom in His Path in Thy Presence, Oh Thou in whose Hand is the Kingdom of all things. And verily Thou art the Almighty! (Attributed to 'Abdu'l-Bahá, in *Prayers, Tablets, Instructions and Miscellany*, p. 19)

We can never fully understand the power service can behold, until we go somewhere and see our actions flourish. It is amazing how one's actions can affect another human being.

So why am I a Bahá'í? I feel I am a Bahá'í to let people know that there will be lots of difficulties in one's life and there will be times when you will question your faith. I am here to tell you that those difficulties are essential to your growth, not only as a human being, but also spiritually. At present I have forgiven my perpetrator because as a Bahá'í we are asked to strive to forgive. I know that he will be judged in the next realm, so why hold onto all that hate? That will not do anything but hurt me more.

I hope this story helps you in any way it can. Alláh-u-Abhá my dear friends!

In His Service,
Kai

~~~~~~~~~~

Anonymous

As for me, let's just say I'm a 22-year-old world citizen pioneering in Eastern Europe.

I grew up in an abusive Bahá'í family. People sometimes ask me how that's possible, when the Bahá'í teachings speak so strongly against abuse. The only answer I have for that is that people do not become perfect the moment that they recognize God and invite Him into their lives. It's not much of an answer, and perhaps it's an overly excusing one, but it's the best I have for now. People also ask why I stay with the Faith after all that's been done to me, with all the problems I've had with the Faith, and I don't always have a good answer for that either.

I stay because I haven't found anything better. I stay because I can't become a Christian and wait for Jesus to return when I believe that Jesus has returned. Judaism appeals to me, but I guess not enough to actually convert. For the most part, I try to separate the Faith I love from the believers who are, at best, imperfect. After all, no matter what church or religious community I'd look at, I'm sure I'd find imperfect believers there: good people, bad people, people trying hard, people not trying at all.

Still, because of the way I was abused, good and evil have become so entangled in my mind that I fear it will be my life's work to untangle them. Many of the good teachings were perverted by the people who abused me, so that when I look at them, I see the original intent, yes, but I also see the darkness and it's a constant struggle.

I went pioneering about five years back, because I wasn't sure what to do with myself after high school and Eastern Europe looked interesting. I'm still here, mostly because we have a wonderful Bahá'í community here, very warm and alive, and going to the Bahá'í meetings feels like coming to a place I could call 'home'.

I didn't know much of the language when I moved here, so I had to learn it. Reading Bahá'í prayers really helped my vocabulary. I'm just about fluent now and so I'm involved with translation efforts. I started translating because there weren't any children's books available, no Bahá'í bedtime stories for my little friends, and if I thought too hard about that it made me cry, so I had to do something about it. There are now about ten children's books available. I watch with pride as my seven-year-old friend reads them aloud to herself.

Our community has devotional gatherings on Tuesdays, Thursdays, Saturdays and Sundays. I go to as many as I can, even though the Saturday one requires a half hour bus ride. I go early for that one because I'm doing a Ruhi study circle with the lady who lives there. We're doing it together, with her tutoring me, because I wanted to do Ruhi book 4 and I didn't want to wait a couple years for it. After Ruhi and after the prayers I play Barbies with my seven-year-old friend.

Once my little friend was singing one of the Hidden Words and I asked her what she thought it meant. I quoted a sentence from it that I thought was relatively simple but she said she didn't know. I asked her to guess and she said she really didn't know, so I started writing a book that helps children to analyse prayers through asking questions. It's nearly finished. I suppose when I'm done I'll translate it into English.

Out of the whole prayer book, there are very few prayers I can say without feeling bad for one reason or another. Most of this stems from the abuse. There are also a few that I'm shy about saying in public and prefer to say alone. There are also a few prayers that I prefer to say alone, not because of the content but because I can't pronounce some of the words with my English accent and the way I pronounce them turns them into swear words. Since I can't help my accent (believe me, I've tried), I prefer to say those prayers only when I'm alone rather than mispronounce them in public.

One problem was that I couldn't keep track of a hundred

prayers in my head and often started reading one at a prayer meeting, only to get to a triggery part at the end and find I barely had enough oxygen to finish it!

So one night I decided I was going to make little notes next to all of the prayers in my prayer book, something small and unobtrusive that would call my attention to different aspects of the prayer so that I would know what I was getting myself into before I started reading it out loud. It took several days but I made it through the entire prayer book, underlining bits with coloured pencil and colouring the number above each prayer according to a code I devised: red is triggery, yellow is especially beautiful, green is safe, light blue is for the prayers I don't feel worthy of saying, dark blue for lines I find problematic but not triggery and purple for prayers I want to say alone. Most prayers are marked with more than one colour.

I now mostly say the green and yellow ones at prayer meetings, saving the purple ones for when I'm at home and the red ones for when I'm feeling okay enough to handle them. Every now and then I take one of the red prayers and deepen on it in writing – sentence by sentence writing a response to it to help me work through it. Some Bahá'ís have said that they used to label the pretty prayers but then they only read those and later on realized that all the prayers were beautiful. I agree with that sentiment but my labelling system is a lot more elaborate than that and it's in place to make it possible for me to pray without being daunted by opening the prayer book, for fear I might stumble on the landmines within.

There's one prayer which I find especially beautiful. I often used to start out reading it in prayer meetings because the words were so pretty, and then I'd get to the last lines – 'Verily, Thou art the helper of the weak and the defender of the little ones' ('Abdu'l-Bahá, in *Bahá'í Prayers*, p. 217) – by which time it was too late to take it back. My whole body would go numb, I'd struggle for breath and I'd go home feeling terrible and have flashbacks when I fell asleep. Now that I have a warning system in place, I know that I can open my prayer book without fear. I still sometimes have problems when someone else says a triggery prayer and that I can't avoid. I certainly couldn't justify to myself telling our community to read only a tiny portion of prayers in my presence. I don't feel it's my place to do so, so I cope and don't say anything. Sometimes at the end of the prayer meeting the back of my hand is red from teeth marks, though I don't remember biting my hands.

Would it be easier to leave? Probably, but I believe God sent Bahá'u'lláh as the messenger of God for this day. I believe in the holy writings. If I didn't, it would be easier to leave but I believe and that makes it hard.

That's okay. Faith isn't supposed to make things easier. Religion isn't about being comfortable.

Would it be easier to stop believing in God entirely? Probably, but whenever I see a spider's web, I see a creature with a brain the size of an ant creating a masterpiece with perfectly proportioned lines and angles. Whenever I square numbers in my head to calm myself down I think about how I know 43 x 43 is 1849 but also that there was Someone a long time before people existed who put all the numbers in order and made them squareable, and that makes me happy. And when I see my toaster I think about who made it possible for rocks to be turned into metal, through some mysterious and magical process which I know very little about; but I know that God gave that attribute to the rocks and let us figure it out. Once when I was flying the clouds looked like land and the sky looked like little rivers and ponds and waterfalls flowing through the clouds and God created that too. I think it would be very difficult not to believe in God with all these signs all around me. I also think that if I managed to convince myself that it wasn't God but rather randomness that created these things, I'd be all that more amazed.

So I'm stuck. I'm a Bahá'í because I believe and because I can't stop believing; and because when I read stories from the *Dawnbreakers* it makes me cry; and when I read *The Priceless Pearl* about all that Shoghi Effendi accomplished, that makes me cry; and when I read *The Chosen Highway* I also feel moved to tears and that's because I believe.

Sometimes I wonder whether I do much good or not because I've been so affected by the aftermath of the abuse, the post-traumatic stress and the depression and other ensuing illnesses that I can, at times, barely take care of myself, let alone serve others. But I try and I go to school and I talk about religion with my friends when the topic comes up. I do my translations, I work with the junior youth, I go to Ruhi classes and attend LSA meetings. I hold devotional meetings in my home and hope that this makes up for all the things I can't do, for the days I sit at home and cry and don't manage to get to the grocery store for food; and all the basic things I know I could be doing if I had my mental health, if all the hurts in my fragmented soul didn't prevent me from understanding the writings better. If, if, if – but I do what I can and maybe someday when I'm old and frail and getting ready to move on I'll have redeemed myself.

Chelsea Gifford

Chelsea Gifford, 20 at the time of writing, is probably the luckiest girl alive. She was born in Kentucky to a family of good-hearted and funny people and grew up half with them and half in the arms of Nancy Campbell Collegiate Institute in Stratford, Ontario, under the guidance of a community of dedicated and caring individuals to whom she feels she owes just about everything except her socks and shoes. She has had the great blessing of participating in service projects both nationally and internationally and learning from all of the Bahá'ís and Bahá'í communities she has had the pleasure of being acquainted with over the years. She is currently back in the bluegrass studying to be a midwife and public health administrator, with plans to further her study of the Mandarin language and dumplings next year while in China teaching English.

This imperfect smat of words is what I have to give.

It was inspired by a verse attributed to 'Abdu'l-Bahá in which He refers to people passing in and out of a garden and how some 'remain for life' to tend it.

This piece is dedicated to Ellen Naylor, who taught me the meaning of 'walking the spiritual path with practical feet'.

Life in the Garden

You lean over the gate and ask, what is life like in the garden?

Why do you stay?

Because the proofs surround me on all sides. Look over my shoulder; plants grow stronger taller, and bear more luscious fruits when cultivated.

I've known the wilderness; my heart has been broken by the sight of plants that never bloom, the competition, the chaos, the smell of rotting fruit. Every beautiful thing I saw out there is magnified here in the garden. While things here are not perfect, this is the best proposal I have heard for the transformation of the landscape. Who doesn't hold in their heart the hope of Eden?

Still, there are snakes in the garden. There are thistles and weeds and acres and acres that have yet to be touched. Life is not easy, in fact trying to live here is the hardest thing I have ever done. The hardest thing I do. Everyday. It never gets any easier. The challenges that it poses, however, do not compare to the exhaustion induced by trying to grow unaided outside. For that, and for the joy, I stay.

I believe that within this place I have found my authentic vocation; for me it was as easy to recognize as the roundness of an orange placed in your palm. I have found that heeding the Gardener causes me to be saturated in sun, and when I suppose I might know better, or know more, and follow my own advice, I usually end up mucking things up. For me, this is proof enough. I have seen how this plan, these tools, which are so capably suited for this climate, work, and that is enough to garner my respect, admiration and life's energies.

The dreams of my heart are simple: that everyone has an opportunity to grow up safe and nourished and 'appear in the utmost beauty'. In the garden there is not only a plan to accomplish that but there is also help. I stay because I love that. I stay because I am of better use here. I stay because there is so much work to be done. I stay because this patch of land is the home of hope.

A WARM PLACE IN MY HEART

Daniel Jones

Daniel Jones teaches children's classes in Ottawa, Canada, and tinkers around with web sites for a living. The youngest son of a family of Bahá'í pioneers, he was bitten by the pioneering bug himself after the Sherbrooke Youth Congress in July 2001. He has blogged about his various service experiences since 2002 at pizza.sandwich.net.

> Entering upon that path you will make an end of pain. Having learnt the removal of thorns, have I taught you the path.
>
> *Buddha*

It was the day of Naw-Rúz and a mighty storm had blown in, coating the roads, hills and fields with a thick blanket of snow. Unsure whether or not he had left, his friends called to check up on him. 'You must still be around,' came the voices over the answering machine. 'Who would leave to pioneer in weather like this? Call us when you get back in,' they said. And down the road, turning the corner onto the highway, there he was, in his father's beat-up 11-year-old car, advancing into a blinding expanse of white.

He had brought very little – a suitcase full of clothes, a suit, a bag full of resumés, newspapers and the writings of Bahá'u'lláh. He roamed this way and that throughout the town, walking into downtown shops and asking if they were hiring – without much luck. For the first week, he stayed with an older couple, two Bahá'ís whose grown children were living in the big city. After the week was up, he returned home for another week to pack the rest of his belongings and say goodbye to his family.

As he rolled back down the road to settle into the city that would be his home for the next year, he wondered, how often does the average soul find itself feeling lost in life? Although he was generally following a path and had a vague sense of goals, he didn't know where following this path or pursuing these goals would take him. The decision to leave home for a year of service came from a longing desire somewhere deep inside him, a desire he didn't really understand. He knew where he was, physically. He wasn't quite as sure where he was spiritually and he was even less sure where he would end up. He had read the Bahá'í writings and marvelled at the concepts he found therein; to him it seemed like a foregone conclusion that the object of his longing would be found through living the Bahá'í life. But he felt keenly aware of how far he was from fulfilling Bahá'í ideals. They seemed so distant from him that he felt lost and confused, like a wanderer lost in the wilderness straining to hear the cry 'Here am I. Here am I', barely even sure what his next step would be.

He had never been strongly involved in the life of the Bahá'í community, a fact that left him feeling down and somewhat ashamed. His parents had been Bahá'ís since the 1960s and had spent over ten years as pioneers; his sister had already spent time overseas to serve the Faith. He knew that he wasn't living his life to the fullest of his capacity and that his spiritual life – indeed, his own connection to God – left much to be desired. He was fresh out of university and now the time seemed right for a kick in the butt, so why not apply for a year of service? Things would turn out all right. As long as he tried to have some faith in God and as long as he had food for the week and a roof over his head, he would be safe. He could handle it, he thought – it would be a challenge. He could take care of himself. Answers and guidance would come gradually, he thought, and more would be revealed.

The Bahá'í institutions responsible for the area had decided to direct him towards a community that needed one more person to form its Local Spiritual Assembly, given that he was of age – he had recently celebrated his twenty-second birthday. The community had played host to Bahá'í pioneers for at least the last ten years and he was the last one needed to give birth to one of the basic institutions of Bahá'í community life. On the first day of Riḍván that year, in a highly anticipated and joyous celebration, the Spiritual Assembly was finally formed, prompting a flood of glad-tidings sent by email and phone to the entire regional Bahá'í community.

Among the key features of service, he had been told before leaving his home community, are the tests that inevitably come along with it. He was reminded of the clear and repeated warnings of 'Abdu'l-Bahá, who, according to Shoghi Effendi, 'laid stress on the "severe mental tests" that would inevitably sweep over His loved ones of the West – tests that would purge, purify and prepare them for their noble mission in life'. (Shoghi Effendi, *Bahá'í Administration*, p. 50) As the year continued, he began to experience the full force of these tests. He moved from apartment to apartment several times, trying unsuccessfully in the meantime to find a permanent job. Things were just beginning to look up as he was offered a four-month contract to work at his service post – and then, of course, came car troubles. His father's 11-year-old car, already on its second engine, had seen its final days. Scrambling, he soon found a new car to use – but less than a month later it was totalled in a car accident during an evening of harsh freezing rain. Unhurt but deeply shaken, he returned to his service, managing to find yet another car to take him to and from his new place of work. He could handle it, he kept on repeating to himself. He could take care of himself.

Time continued to pass and the pace of life never stopped. Stubbornly unused to asking for help, he began to feel exhausted trying to keep up with the increasing demands of work and service. When he wasn't at work, he was at an Assembly meeting, visiting isolated believers, acting as a tutor for study circles or helping to plan regional youth conferences – either that or paying bills and keeping his car tuned up. He was confronted with living an entirely new life and he was having trouble dealing with the added stress that came with it. One would think he would have slowed down, waited until the end of his year of service and gone home. But deep down he felt his purpose hadn't been achieved – whatever he had come out here to fix, it still wasn't fixed. So when in the spring, near the end of his year of service, a call went out from the Regional Bahá'í Council to form a new Spiritual Assembly in a neighbouring town, he jumped at the chance and made plans to move into the town. Seeing as a Bahá'í couple had recently moved into his adopted community – making more than the required nine adult Bahá'ís needed to elect the Assembly – he felt he might have a second chance at this new post. Perhaps, he felt, he might do it right this time.

The newness of the experience brought him some temporary joy but soon the stress returned. It was even harder for him to find a job in this new post, so he kept himself busy in the meantime by volunteering. There were fewer Bahá'ís in the new town, so there was no chance of forming a Spiritual Assembly that year; instead, they waited for new believers to declare or for new pioneers to arrive. He began to realize that instead of lifting, the creeping feeling of depression that had come over him after his recent car accident was building. Even after he was offered a new contract he was feeling more tired than happy. As a youth in his large, well-established home community, he had never been exposed to the type of problems faced by fledgling Bahá'í communities – and he had certainly never been asked to take an active role in confronting and fixing them! Yet there he was, in the thick of it, feeling the weight of the responsibility that comes with pioneering and serving on Bahá'í institutions. He kept on praying – trying to squeeze every last drop of spirituality out of those prayers, prayers he was still trying desperately to understand. He had already taken on the role of group secretary, with its attendant responsibilities; then came the extra responsibility of acting as Area Coordinator for the local cluster's Bahá'í Institute. Stubborn as ever, he still asked for no help – he could take care of himself, he thought. Despite his mounting exhaustion, he repeated to himself that he could take it.

Finally, after months of hard work and service, the Christmas holidays came around and he decided to go back to his hometown to visit his family. It was going to be great. He got up early that morning, packed his bags, loaded them into his car and set out towards the highway on his way back home. He was still reeling and high-strung from the stress of work – not to mention all that correspondence, oh, and the meeting he had just driven back from last night – but already he was starting to get into his holidays. He thought of seeing his parents and family once again after such a while, of having a nice, relaxing holiday and a well-deserved pause from an arduous period of service. He thought of how good it would be to be back among all the friends he had grown up with in the Bahá'í community at home. In fact, he thought of just about everything but the weather. Within seconds of getting onto the highway, he was already being pelted by thick snow and ice but he pressed on. He was barely 10 or 15 minutes down the road when his car begin to slide. With an expression of blank horror on his face, he watched as his little car swerved towards the snowbank at the side of the road, spun out and flipped onto its side, mere inches from the cars and trucks speeding down the highway.

In the Qur'án, the holy book of Islam, it is written 'Think men that when they say "We believe" they shall be let alone and not be put to proof?' (Qur'án 29:1) Declaring one's belief in a Manifestation of God, identifying oneself with a particular religion, is a powerful act. It releases tremendous spiritual potential in one's own life and in the lives of those we know and love. But is it all we need to do in order to fulfil our commitment to God? Bahá'u'lláh opens His Most Holy Book, the Kitáb-i-Aqdas, with a statement of two inseparable duties that apply to all humankind: the first is 'the recognition of Him Who is the Dayspring of His Revelation and the Fountain of His laws' and the second is 'to observe every ordinance of Him Who is the Desire of the world'. These 'twin duties' are so inseparable, Bahá'u'lláh writes, that 'neither is acceptable without the other'. (Bahá'u'lláh, *Kitáb-i-Aqdas*, para 1)

Even so, all too often we find ourselves falling into the trap of complacency, of being satisfied with ourselves – 'satisfied' in the sense of not feeling the need to strive to fulfil our twin duties. But each one of us, no matter how learned, how experienced or how well-off in any sense of the word, will face difficulties in life that will test our strength and our resolve. Shoghi Effendi tells us that we are Bahá'ís because we believe it is the truth for this day and not because of any hopes we may have for an easier passage through this troubled world.

Through trials and tests, man achieves a greater state of perfection and learns how he best should be. 'Abdu'l-Bahá explained this concept by citing examples from nature. 'The plant most pruned by the gardeners', He says, 'is that one which, when the summer comes, will have the most beautiful blossoms and the most abundant fruit. The labourer cuts up the earth with his plough, and from that earth comes the rich and plentiful harvest. The more a man is chastened, the greater is the harvest of spiritual virtues shown forth by him.' ('Abdu'l-Bahá, *Paris Talks*, p. 50)

I met our troubled friend a while back and he seemed a lot

less troubled than his story suggests. Turns out that not long after that incredible accident he hit a pretty big down and got severely depressed, to the point where he was having suicidal thoughts and was unable to function. At that point, he told me, he realized that his life was in the hands of God. Instead of pretending that he was indestructible and that he could handle everything, he said, he gave up his will to God and admitted his powerlessness. He said it was like living the short obligatory prayer – 'I testify, at this moment, to my powerlessness and to Thy might'. (Bahá'u'lláh, in *Bahá'í Prayers*, p. 4) For the first time in his life he went to a friend for help and he ended up going back home to get treated for severe depression. That was the greatest test, he said, because until then he had always imagined that getting therapy and taking medications were signs of weakness. His friend's insistence on Bahá'u'lláh's command to refer to competent physicians in times of sickness, along with lots of prayer, helped him through it. He eventually discovered that he had been suffering with depression for most of his life – which, for him, explained why he felt so lost.

He told me that walking the path of recovery from his depression has brought him closer to Bahá'u'lláh than he has ever been and that it confirmed him in his faith. I must have sounded surprised because he went on to explain further: to see all his best efforts bring him to the breaking point, only to submit to the will of God in the end and be brought back to life, was proof to him of the potency of Bahá'u'lláh's Revelation and the grandeur of His station.

We keep in touch every so often now. In fact, I met him again not too long ago. He had recently been on pilgrimage and we talked all about it. He showed me photos and told stories of the pilgrimage and how it had touched him to learn how much Bahá'u'lláh had suffered during His life. The sufferings my friend went through were nothing compared to the 40 years' imprisonment and exile that Bahá'u'lláh was forced to endure. He quoted a passage that was read during his pilgrimage regarding the sufferings of Bahá'u'lláh:

> The Ancient Beauty hath consented to be bound with chains that mankind may be released from its bondage, and hath accepted

to be made a prisoner within this most mighty Stronghold that the whole world may attain unto true liberty. He hath drained to its dregs the cup of sorrow, that all the peoples of the earth may attain unto abiding joy, and be filled with gladness. (Bahá'u'lláh, *Gleanings*, p. 99)

I was going to ask him what the quotation meant to him but I think I figured it out.

Chloë Filson

Chloë Filson graduated with a BA in English Literature from Trent University in Peterborough, Ontario in the spring of 2007. She worked for Trent's English Department as a facilitator for a second-year English course. She was a three-time first place poetry winner of the annual Spirit within Art Show at Trent University. Chloë is an avid Scrabble player and likes honey in her tea.

Rungs
or Meditation on Music and the Long Obligatory Prayer
2 April 2006

I am a stranger
Hastening to my home
Beneath this canopy of clouds,
Beyond this canopy of clouds.

Will my words reach out
Like your song did?
Your song reached in.
Who am I to write words?

I am this transgressor
Seeking the absolvent ocean,
The salt water of His forgiveness

Lapping these wounds.
I am this pillar dissolving.

His Pen brings the words to my soul
His words bring the power to my pen
Your song brings His power to my heart

A prayer is
A song is
A longing,
A ladder.
The words that you sung –
Those words are the rungs.
Who am I that I should dare to climb?
Who am I that I should dare not to climb?

I am this lowly one
Seeking His holy court
Who am I to have heard?
Who am I to write words?

I am this poor creature
Created
Creating

Who am I, otherwise?

Angus Cowan Epp

Angus was born in Saskatchewan in 1988 to a Bahá'í family but has lived for most of his life in British Columbia. Born with muscular dystrophy, Angus has two older brothers, Seamus and Salim, who passed away from muscular dystrophy in 1992.

It's good to have something to believe in because you need something to motivate you to keep doing good things in life, like being kind to others and making the world a better place.

By helping others you help yourself.

When I help others it helps me feel positive about myself and helps me know that I can do good things in my life. Sometimes when you help, you receive help, too.

An example of making the world a better place: I play electric wheelchair soccer – Powersoccer – for a team in Surrey, B.C. I've been to tournaments in Atlanta, Georgia; San Jose, California; and Mesa, Arizona, as well as tournaments in B.C. I've played for eight years. In team sports I can be a role model for younger players and teach them how to be sportsmanlike and help them develop new skills.

Powersoccer also makes it possible for me to become good at something and that helps improve my self-image and inspires me to believe that I can make a difference in the world. It's another example of the power of believing in something.

Luke (Ahkivgak) Baumgartner

My name is Ahkivgak Baumgartner. I am also called Luke. I am from Barrow, Alaska. My parents are Bahá'ís and my father's parents are Bahá'ís, so through my paternal ancestry I am a third generation Bahá'í. My grandparents pioneered to Alaska throughout the '50s and '60s. My father, who had left, returned to Barrow, recently married, in 1970 as a pioneer. He left Barrow in 2001–2002 to serve on the NSA of Alaska, bringing the family with him. I was born in 1980 and I spent my first 12 years in Barrow and (roughly) the next six at Maxwell International Bahá'í School. I am Inupiat (Northern Alaskan Inuit) and white.

Right Living

Isolated and distinct: these words best describe my social experience in Barrow. As Bahá'ís we were distinct from virtually everyone. Racial tensions existed and I was sometimes on one side or the other. My parents, for all their good work, for reasons that were perhaps wise, held themselves fairly apart from the community at large. I recall feeling quite isolated, with few people to relate to. I would presume that this was not an unusual experience for Bahá'í youth. This isolationism was exacerbated by the fact that at this point the Inupiat people of Barrow were primarily Christian and the leaders of the churches at various times directly preached against the Bahá'í Faith. The point of all this is that I was constantly reminded of my identity as a Bahá'í and as a person occupying a cultural cusp from a very young age, before one is required to investigate independently or has the tools necessary to do so. My explicit meaning is that my early experience was that my family, and the family down the road, *were* the Bahá'í Faith. I did not, and likely could not, understand the questions involved in the nature of reality and, further, the reality of the Bahá'í Faith. I could not define the Faith as an entity distinct from these people that I interacted with on a daily basis, which, although not a complete understanding, is a necessary one.

Later on, I went to Maxwell. Certainly I brought similar misconceptions to this school. It was, after all, a Bahá'í school. As I understood it, school and the Faith were one and the same. It was the physical manifestation of so much talk and reading. I survived this experience without withdrawing from the Faith. Some of my friends there did not. I tend to be tenacious about certain things and I think that although during this period I was not particularly confirmed in my Faith, I did not withdraw because I failed to find any reason significant enough to impel me to withdraw. The question I am getting to is, why would a person raised in a staunch Bahá'í family, well-known throughout Alaska, sent at great cost to a private Bahá'í school, have such a hard time accepting the Faith? I have never been alone, immersed in a secular experience. There were always Bahá'í individuals and communities in my life.

Recently, I ran across an explanation I particularly appreciated, from former House of Justice member Adib Taherzadeh:

> The Cause of God is exalted above the world of humanity. In order to embrace it, man must acquire divine qualities. Here, self and worldly ambitions become great barriers. The test of man, therefore, is to subdue his own self. Without this he cannot recognize the Prophet. For the Manifestation of God has two natures, the divine and the human. The former is always hidden by the latter. Only those who have spiritual eyes can penetrate through the veil of human limitations and behold the reality of the Manifestation. Those who are spiritually blind are tested by the personality of the Prophet. They can see only the human qualities and often seek to find fault with these Holy Souls.
>
> After recognition of the Manifestation, the believer will be tested by God in many ways. Each time he passes a test, he will acquire greater spiritual insight and will grow stronger in faith. The closer he gets to the person of the Manifestation the more difficult become his tests. It is then that any trace of ambition or ego may imperil his spiritual life. (Taherzadeh, *Revelation of Bahá'u'lláh*, vol. 1, p. 129)

Unlike the early believers, who were quite often pious and outstanding scholars who had spent a lifetime struggling with matters of faith, Bahá'í children must face up to these challenges from the moment they become aware of the Faith. They have not chosen the Faith. They do not understand it. Nonetheless, they experience the tests referred to above. They cannot see – and I personally found it extremely challenging – the divine in the mundane operations and the myriad mistakes of fledgling Bahá'í institutions (including Bahá'í families). I would furthermore charge that few, if any, Bahá'í institutions involving children and youth could be characterized as 'mature'.

There is an argument that external forces are also responsible for withdrawal from the Faith. Taherzadeh alludes to them as 'self and worldly ambitions'. As much as this may be the case, it is not something that we really can do a whole lot about. We cannot expect non-Bahá'ís to follow Bahá'í laws and live according to Bahá'í principles. Nor can we, except by our own actions, change our social environment.

A few personal reflections: When I was around ten years of age I recall being introduced to the notion of a standard of behaviour, applied to me by my parents. Mostly, I simply looked to see whether or not my parents lived by the standard they were attempting to impart unto me. In my particular circumstance, I had no reason to expect anything less than full compliance with the standard as it was held up to me. Naturally, none of my family, including myself, in my eyes, met this standard. As I referred to above, this sort of thing extended throughout my years at Maxwell. When I talk to people who have withdrawn from the Faith or have had some experience with the Faith but were not attracted to it, the reason for their distance is invariably a dissatisfaction with some perceived failure of behaviour, action or simply a bad experience with an individual or institution of the Bahá'í Faith. They have rarely given the matter any critical investigation or thought.

In my opinion, there is no justification for abandoning the Faith on the basis of logical or doctrinal grounds. The responsible scholar will investigate the matter fully and independently enough. If we object to a Bahá'í tenet 'as we heard it from someone', we are objecting to that person. We can appreciate the accomplishments of Bahá'í individuals without requiring their perfection. There are many Bahá'í writings which have perplexed and challenged me personally. When I can't figure something out, I file it away in my mind. As I receive new information, a new understanding or a life experience, these lead me to grasp the problem again and I reexamine my understanding. Individuals with objections to personalities, family or institutions may attempt to mask their objection with 'logic' or 'argument' but few North American young people will really study these topics until well into higher education. I know I didn't. Fewer still will genuinely grasp them.

If we reject the Faith based on a problem we have with it right now, we are presuming that no new understanding will be reached by us in the course of our lifetime. Furthermore, there are mysteries related to many religions which were not unravelled until Bahá'u'lláh explained them. To expect that we, as individuals, will comprehend the meaning of Bahá'u'lláh's Revelation in its entirety, at this very moment, is absurd. I find, typically, that individuals who turn away from the Faith but then attempt to justify their decision based on any kind of reasoning are not open to investigation, criticism and analysis. We must be open to all considerations, including religion, and whatever it is we personally may find distasteful. Certainly there are many religionists who have chosen not to face question and criticism. But I also find that many people who claim to be open-minded, who claim to be progressive and claim to be critical, are simply not. They refuse criticism, refuse investigation and refuse to consider alternative viewpoints, whether religious or not. At the heart of it, we are all people of faith. The question becomes, what do these individuals who turn away from the Bahá'í Faith have faith in?

I did eventually investigate a few other avenues of living, and a significant reason for living as a Bahá'í was that all of these other ways of living failed to compare to the Bahá'í Faith. Many I enjoyed and appreciated, and still do, but few have the encompassing vision that the Bahá'í Faith does, and if they do, they lack any kind of systematic plan of action. For me, all other avenues failed. The good things I hoped for in life came about only as a result of ways of living contained within the Bahá'í framework. I also examined periods of my life where I drifted away from the Faith. Was the outcome good? Did it, in fact, make me happy? I experienced some fleeting enjoyments but for the most part I felt lost, alone and unhappy.

I appreciated and valued other religions but they were too small for me; they did not face the immenseness of the world, preferring to face only what was within a very clearly defined framework. I enjoy logic and philosophy but it is very clear to me that if we base our faith on some kind of personal 'proof' or system of logic or argument, if someone or something comes along that defeats that argument, our faith is defeated with it. Faith is not something that can be 'proved' in a personal sense. That's why it's faith. Other religions are contained within the Bahá'í Faith. It was like, yep, that's there but that's not enough by itself. I finally felt all the good things that I hoped for in life: a happy family, individual strength, integrity and courage, happiness and love. All those things, and more, I found were simply abandoned, undermined and corrupted by selfish pursuits. I learned about progression, I learned to forgive myself for mistakes and therefore to forgive others for theirs. I considered my attitudes and challenged my perceptions and beliefs. I lamented my bewilderment and impotence to assuage the suffering and pain evident in every corner of life I ever investigated. I finally concluded that the best hope for all and everything at this time, including me, was the Bahá'í Faith.

This conclusion was a freedom of sorts. I investigated other religions and found that they assisted me immensely in understanding my own religion. Philosophy and logic assisted me in meeting the corrupt and faulty arguments of popular culture, including those in less rigorous academic settings. I began to understand that things were a process; that if something did not make sense to me now it might in the future; that the notion that everything in the Faith would meet with our full approval, that there would be some kind of snug smugness, was a faulty one. Past religions were never fully understood until the passage of time and the explications of Bahá'u'lláh. Should we expect anything less? That we, as individuals, will master the mysteries and understandings of Bahá'u'lláh's Revelation? Certainly this topic is a massive one and I think that I have only glossed over a few points. I think that what we need to do to convince youth raised as Bahá'ís to become Bahá'ís is simply to live in accordance with Bahá'u'lláh's teachings. Suffering, sacrifice, strength. It's not really that complicated, just really hard. If you do that and others still choose not to become Bahá'ís, leave it in Bahá'u'lláh's hands.

After all, it's not really 'us' who attract people to the Faith. The dual nature referred to above by Taherzadeh must lead us to question the existence of a 'self'. The source of attraction is divine. People are not attracted to 'me', they are attracted to the divine qualities reflected in my character and actions. We don't want our young people to love 'us'. This will lead them away from the Faith. Taherzadeh notes the examples of certain early believers very close to Bahá'u'lláh who later became covenant-breakers. We want people to love the divine, love Bahá'u'lláh and to love God. If they do this our mistakes will be met with understanding and forgiveness, instead of bitterness and rejection.

Nysa Pilbrow

Nysa Pilbrow was raised in Haifa, the child of a French-Canadian mother and an English-Canadian father. She graduated from Nancy Campbell Collegiate Institute in Stratford, Ontario, went on to a year of service in Ecuador, began university at Queen's, in Kingston, Ontario, and wrote from Ecuador during an exchange year while studying abroad. She makes her home in Gatineau, Quebec, with her parents when she is not travelling for the Bahá'í Faith.

I never became a Bahá'í, really. By the time I had the mind to grasp somewhat what the Faith was, I was already well nested in the heart of the Faith. I grew up in Haifa and the Faith was all around me. By the time I understood that I had a choice as to whether or not I wanted to be a Bahá'í I was already so convinced of its truth that the choice was irrelevant. It was not a decision I had to consider at great length. In reality, there was no difference between the day before I declared and the day after. It was as if I was telling a long-time loved one how much I cared for him. It was obvious; it had already been expressed. Life moved on.

I do not think I started to be Bahá'í for real until I left Haifa at the age of 16. This is not to say that I was not a Bahá'í before, but once I left Haifa, practising the laws of the Faith became a conscious choice rather than a conditioned behaviour. I finished my last two years of high school at Nancy Campbell, the Bahá'í-inspired school in southern Ontario. I used Nancy Campbell as a buffer zone between Haifa and the rest of the world, a transitional space, a gateway community, a safe house. But it's easy to be a Bahá'í in a Bahá'í environment. I spent a 'year of service', a kind of rite-of-passage for many Bahá'í youth.

Mine was spent walking on eggshells in an indigenous community in Ecuador. I did Ruhi classes, worked in a school, had children's classes and discovered that if you are Caucasian and religious, people will often equate you with every other white missionary that has ever crossed their path. It was hard to break that barrier.

When I came back to Canada I fell off the boat. I can guarantee you that for every youth who returns from a year of service inspired there is one who returns (or soon becomes) depressed. I found that university had so little to offer. My professors were answering all of the wrong questions. The Faith seemed so irrelevant to the rest of the world. All of a sudden all religions blended into one and I could not tell the difference between Bahá'í devotionals and Christian prayer gatherings, a year of service and missions, Ruhi and the Alpha courses. I knew there was a difference but I could not vocalize it to anyone. At the same time I was meeting all of these wonderful people who were not Bahá'ís and who were far more marvellous, service oriented, kind and pure than I could ever aspire to be. And soon enough the Great North American Question began to haunt me: Why do we even need religion?

As I write, I'm in a hostel in the Ecuadorian Andes. I'm here on a year exchange through my school's international development programme. I've returned to my year of service post with an academic rather than religious purpose and now it's time for me to reconcile those two worlds. I just got out of a meeting in which my academic counsellor asked me my views regarding development. I tried to explain the important role a spiritual education can play in social and economic development. I jumbled my words and sounded more like an idealistic naive do-gooder than anyone who actually deserved her time of day. I was shot down like a bird in hunting season.

So, being a Bahá'í can make you feel alone. But then again, all 27 members of my programme know that I'm a Bahá'í and have something of an idea of what that means. Last night we made a giant pot of spaghetti for a communal dinner – they all decided to make the whole batch without wine so that I would be able to eat it, even though I am the only one who does not drink. I woke up on my second day here to find my roommate reading a Hidden Words that someone had given her back home. Most of the others already have some Bahá'í friends and are willing to talk openly about faith, belief, religion and spirituality.

I have no intention of leaving this programme with x number of new Bahá'ís. There is no race to find new Bahá'ís. But you can be sure that they will all know what the Bahá'í Faith is by the time we are done here.

Juliette Lord

Juliette Lord is an alumnus of Maxwell International Bahá'í School on Vancouver Island, Canada, year of '99. Married to Nabil Naderi, whom she met in high school, she has travelled extensively as a Bahá'í teacher. In addition to being a dancer, she is a poet, artist and singer and is deeply committed to humanitarian issues. As of January 2007 Juliette and Nabil are proud parents of a son.

March 2005

First a little bit about me: I am 23 years old and I have been married for two and a half years. I was born in Douglasville, Georgia but I have spent a good many years of my life in Canada and went to boarding school on Vancouver Island. I have a flare for the dramatic. I tend to be very hard on myself but find it necessary in order to keep progressing at a recognizable rate. I think I'm generally a good person, although I am sometimes very confused. By confused I mean spiritually . . . and this will lead me into why I am a Bahá'í.

This is an interesting question. Because if I were to live the way I want I would probably not be a Bahá'í. Especially not lately. I want to drink. I want to feel guiltless when I swear. I want to be brash and mean to people I don't like. I want to hole myself up in my house because I am scared of the world. Although all these feelings run counter to the teachings of the Faith, I have not left it in order to explore them guilt free. And although I am so tempted by these things, I still walk against their tide and try not to be swept away by them. The fact of the matter is, it would be incredibly stupid for me to leave the Faith just to follow my petty temptations. It has given me so much. Every positive thing in my life has some connection to the Bahá'í Faith and is there as a result of my relationship with it.

I am still a Bahá'í today because I feel there is truth in the Faith. I believe it is the closest thing to truth I have found in this world. I believe that when I meditate, as the Faith tells me to do, I find truth. And when I find a little sliver of truth, it always guides me through the pressing situation at hand. The truth of the Faith can guide all sorts of people who need it in all sorts of situations. It is universally applicable throughout the ages and across a diversity of people. And as much as I don't want to admit it, I truly feel the Faith is the only thing that can ultimately help people and humanity to find safe footing into the future.

I have tried to cut Bahá'u'lláh out of my life and see if I could find truth in other places but I always feel there is no guidance anywhere without Him. Or I feel that the best advice I could follow is the advice He has already given me in His writings. I try to be self-sufficient and declare that I am independent of God. When I do, I can't help but realize that it is the years of striving to live in accordance with the laws of the Bahá'í Faith that has made me so happy. Striving to be noble, as the Faith tells me I am, made me such a self-assured teenager. This in turn caused me to make so many decisions that were good for me. It caused me to be detached enough from the opinions of others to decide for myself who and when I would date and how the relationship would go. It was this detachment from immediate gratification that allowed me to marry my husband only when I felt that every cell of my body was prepared and consented to marry him after long and thoughtful consideration, and not to follow my heart or my desires on a whim. The Faith cultivated in me the qualities that my husband loves.

The Faith is the great mediator between myself and the world.

The only reason I do not scream at the person who is being horrible to me is because I have learned by reading the writings, and by practising them in my daily life, that there are better ways to deal with conflict, ways that resonate with positive results. Many times I feel like I don't agree with something the Faith says. But I never feel that the Faith has faulty reasoning. I always attribute my lack of agreement to my inability to understand the true full picture that God has painted for me.

I want to embrace people into my life and I want to be open to everyone. Truly trying to understand the Faith has only made that goal more attainable for me.

The Faith has only given me positive things in my life. It has never been the cause of anything negative whatsoever. It has always been the cause of my growth and maturity. It has never been the cause of my degeneration. Only I have. Only my desire to be accepted or to get something for free or to cut someone else off so that I can get more has caused me pain in my life. Never anything the Faith has ever taught me.

And I apologize that I am not willing to discipline myself to be a much better Bahá'í right now. But I know the Faith is always true. It is like a thread of gold that is timeless. It will never break; it will always be there for me. I can choose to approach it or turn away from it. But it only brings clarity and support to my life.

I have a lot to say about service experiences, conferences, workshops, Ruhi courses, travel, family life and education in the Bahá'í Faith. But I will only give a quick sum up. Of all the items on this list, I would say service is by far the most fun and the most rewarding. I feel that service to the Faith is a very personal call and that no one can translate for you what is the best form of service you can offer. For me, I decide how to serve based on what's needed, what I want to do, and what is not usually given.

I served a lot while at Maxwell. I was in the Dance Workshop. I *loved* being in the Dance Workshop. It was one of the most empowering things I ever have been involved with. We toured all over northern British Columbia to raise awareness about social issues. I feel the positive results of my service with this Workshop were many. The Workshop allowed me to develop healthy friendships with boys around my same age who I could depend on and trust. I also learned a lot about how I wanted my future spouse to treat me and how I wanted to treat him. The Workshop gave me a unique opportunity to meet and connect with people on a sincere level, rather than on a small-talk, superficial one. I think the Workshop also pushed me into a meditative state in which I reflected a lot on my actions and the results of my actions. I thought a lot about how people should be treated and how I want to be remembered. The Workshop gave me an incredible sense of accountability. I think all service does. But above all, it made service fun. My time with the Workshop was one of the most transformative times of my life.

The Bahá'í Faith has caused me to travel. The Faith has essentially made travel an indispensable part of my life. I truly regard the world as my own community because of this. I think this is a huge point. I remember who I am in relation to the world community and don't simply compare my life to my local city or country. I believe that the ability to regard the world as one little home has widened my vision and self-reflection. It has allowed me to make so many more well-informed choices about what is important to me.

I definitely walked around in the murkiness of new waters and sometimes the Faith was like a faint echo in the fog. This was especially true in university. I think getting a spiritual education at Maxwell developed a deep sense of security for me. I'm not glorifying myself, I am trying to glorify the Faith and what it has given me. The Faith has given me amazing tools to deal with daily situations, situations that, once collected, form my life. In university, I felt the Faith was a sounding board for all my new thoughts and feelings. It was a safeguard against total confusion. In university there were a lot of directions to be pulled in. There were so many different groups of people I could have identified myself with. The Faith really helped me feel that I didn't need to align myself with any group of people or follow the politics of my peers. I could choose for myself what I felt I needed and what I would follow and it didn't necessarily have to be one of the many incomplete ideologies presented to me. I could choose 'D' – none of the above. And that was very freeing. Another protection the

Faith provided me in university was an encouragement towards getting to know people and not to gossip too much. OK, gossip is rampant. As someone once told me, 'If you go hang around with smokers you're going to reek with smoke, unless you wash your clothes.' I was not immune. Definitely not. But I do notice that the Faith's encouragement to see the good in people forced me to cross boundaries where others might not have and helped me to be encouraging and loving of my peers.

As far as family life is concerned the Bahá'í Faith has been the great mediator. The Faith emphasizes that we should treat our parents with respect and obey them. I feel that being the person the Faith has encouraged me to be has greatly helped my relationship with my parents. We have issues like anybody but I believe we all make better decisions about how to deal with scary issues than we would without the guidance of the Faith. The Faith also tells women always to 'show' an 'amiable temper' to their husbands. ('Abdu'l-Bahá, in *Compilation*, vol. 1, no. 850, p. 394) I'm sure Nabil would say that I am not always amiable but I try a lot harder as a result of passages like this. The writings encourage me time and time again to try to put away my self and my ego and approach Nabil to resolve a conflict.

Most of the time I am totally terrified to admit to my friends how much I love my Faith. I worry about seeming fanatical just by virtue of being religious. I worry that those around me will be wary that I will try to convert them. My relationship with the Faith isn't all puppy dogs and cotton candy. I am self conscious, usually about what others will think about my religious affiliation, especially given all the horrible things that have happened in the world in the name of religion. But I just have to get over myself and embrace that this is me. Because no matter how many times I analyse dispassionately my position in the world, I always run back towards the Bahá'í Faith with open arms, hungry for the guidance it has to offer me.

The Faith is like my parent, my best friend, my watcher. I do not always give it the love and regard that it deserves but I would be a shell of what I am now without the Faith. I'm a dancer and I am surrounded by girls who have been dancing their whole lives.

Technically, I just started dancing two years ago, so I'm a little behind in that department. But I realize that I have been striving to be a spiritually responsible person for about 17 years. I have studied the techniques of spirituality. Just as these dancers around me have these long, gorgeous, lengthened muscles that they don't have to work for anymore or even think about, just as they have stretched their legs their whole lives to have these amazingly articulate feet and lower limbs, I have been stretching and training my soul because of the Bahá'í Faith. And I am so glad that I have some of those spiritually lengthened muscles that I don't really have to think about so much anymore. And the exciting and sometimes infuriating part is that there is so much more to learn and so much further to go. I feel incredibly lucky to have something so whole to guide me through my life. Maybe one day I will repay God through my good deeds. I don't think I could but I would like to try.

Anyway, wish me luck.

Melodie Cardin

Melodie Cardin was born in 1985 and grew up in a Bahá'í family of Canadian background. She also travelled as a frequent visitor to Belize, where her grandparents were pioneers from 1978 to 2005. She completed a degree in Journalism at Carleton University in Ottawa, Canada in 2007.

My life would be infinitely easier if I were not a Bahá'í.

I have never particularly fitted in among my peers and part of the reason for this has been the higher standard I am called to meet by Bahá'u'lláh. This has manifested itself in all sorts of ways, depending largely on my age. When I was a little girl, it was that over-awed, wide-eyed question, 'You don't celebrate Christmas!?'

Then the third degree would begin. What about presents? Did I believe in Santa Claus? What about Christmas dinner? Did we get turkey? I would explain that we also got presents, we had our own holidays. My friends learned to explain to each other about me . 'Melodie doesn't get presents at Christmas. She gets them at Ayamaka.'[2] I would rarely correct them. I didn't care that people didn't get it. Being a Bahá'í was just another thing that set me apart, like speaking French or moving around a lot.

I now live in the city, and I'm older, and this means there is enough diversity around me that people are no longer so amazed that my religious practices aren't mainstream but I think for some Bahá'ís living in rural areas this problem never goes away.

Most people are very accepting, though, and many have heard good things about the Bahá'í Faith. However, I have met a lot of apathetic people who believe in the culture of fun and don't feel the need for religion. I don't know why I have always felt the need for something deeper than that in my life or why I know without a doubt that God is there and Bahá'u'lláh is His messenger. It seems so remarkably clear to me that I wish I could give that to others. I understand not knowing though. I have heard people's arguments about there not being tangible proof and they're right. The proofs are in the Revelation of Bahá'u'lláh and in the world around me that is so complex and so beautiful I do not think it could have happened by accident. But I understand when people say that God could not exist in a world where unspeakable horrors are allowed to occur. It's hard to understand how a being that is both all powerful and loving could allow these things to occur. I believe that humanity is being allowed to bring tests upon itself because just as individuals need to learn things the hard way, so does humanity and therefore the often horrific state of the world does not do away with my belief in God, although sometimes it can cause doubts.

When I was 11 my family moved to Vancouver Island and I started at Maxwell International Bahá'í School. Maxwell is hard to describe. It is almost another world. It is geographically set apart from other places, not near enough to anything else to be a part of it. It is incredibly sheltered. Maxwell does have the same problems as other high schools . . . sex, drugs, alcohol, cliques. But there's not as much of that . . . and those behaviours can sometimes take

---

[2] The designated Bahá'í period of gift-giving, hospitality and charity, called Ayyám-i-Há, runs from 26 February through 1 March each year.

on a bit of a glamour because of their absence. Being at Maxwell can be like being wrapped up in a big safety blanket, although if I were to say that no one is ever left out, that would be unfair. There are problems at Maxwell like anywhere else but despite them it is much easier to be a Bahá'í there, where so many others are Bahá'ís and it's 'cool' to be Bahá'í. Many youth come out of there feeling incredibly strong and fortified with the Faith, only to quickly crash and burn when faced with the lack of spirituality and insipid culture of their peers away from Maxwell.

I moved to Quebec after three years at Maxwell. I am more thankful than anything that I will never have to repeat the first two years I spent in Quebec. I experienced terrible loneliness. I had found kindred spirits at Maxwell. I believe that if I had stayed there I would have remained friends with those people and they would have been rich friendships. However, my life has become richer because of the loss of them, in a way that is hard to explain. It comes back to my opening statement. My life would be easier if I were not a Bahá'í. In the same way, my life would have been easier if I had stayed at Maxwell, where my tests were something invented and brought upon myself. But I left and lost so much and therefore gained so much.

The Bahá'í Faith has made my relationships more difficult. For starters, holding myself to a higher standard has meant that I hold others to a higher standard too. This is not to say that I always follow Bahá'í law perfectly but it is there, as a guide for me, and I cannot be with anyone who is too far removed from those values. In a way, though, I cannot just blame the difficulty I have had with relationships on the Faith. It's my personality too – I'm really academic and in high school that translates to just plain nerdy. Also, in high school people are not living to their full potential. They allow themselves to be mediocre and because the Bahá'í Faith teaches us to always strive to improve our characters, I had a hard time fitting in.

The loss of friendships through moving has made me wary and I don't trust people as easily, so building new friendships is slow. I know that without the Bahá'í Faith this would have been easier because I could have engaged in the same sorts of things as my peers, mainly drinking and backbiting, and I would have fitted in better. But I need the Faith because that is not the sort of person I want to be anyway and this is why, despite being lonelier, I know that the kinds of friendships I will eventually make will be deeper; so I continue to believe.

I have been lucky in that I have had wonderful experiences but even given that, the Bahá'í Faith is a challenge. I feel that to be with someone who is not also a Bahá'í would mean that that person would miss out on a fundamental part of my being and I wonder how a relationship could then ever be solid. I think about marriage in the future and wonder how I could teach my children the Faith effectively and consult to find solutions to tests if only my half of the marriage was being guided by the Bahá'í writings.

On the other hand, I think it will work out. If Bahá'u'lláh should choose to send me a partner in life who cannot see the fundamental truth I see in the Bahá'í Faith, he will still be guided by God. I believe that we cannot escape being guided by God. This is a blessing but it is also hard work.

It means constant vigilance, from daybreak to sunset. It means that prayers become as habitual as brushing your teeth. While we are all creatures of habit to a certain extent, good habits are hard to develop. It means a level of faith that requires so much energy! We are not allowed to be complacent as Bahá'ís; we are not allowed to be lazy. We are to be constantly striving to develop virtues and better ourselves, and on a day to day basis that can mean a very full day. For my grandparents and aunts, who have been pioneers to Central America, it has meant poverty, hard work and the sacrifice of education and material comforts.

For me it has meant self-denial, self-restraint and getting out of my comfort zone. I struggle against all these things but in the end they will help me become a better person. Every experience of my life has been made fuller and deeper by my knowing the presence of Bahá'u'lláh.

Every thought, every breath, every stupid mistake I've made, every time I've felt lonely, every time I've screwed up, every time I got it right, God is there. You can't run or hide, and although this means my life would be easier if I weren't a Bahá'í, nothing easy is worth having.

A WARM PLACE IN MY HEART

Anisa Qualls

Anisa Qualls comes from a fantastic family and Bahá'í community in Yellow Springs, Ohio. Since graduating from Maxwell International Bahá'í School in 2001 she has explored various kinds of service and attended Earlham College. In December 2006 she received her Bachelor's degree in Latin American Studies. She has been blessed with extraordinary teachers and mentors her entire life and hopes to give those same gifts back through working in education in the years to come.

Stretching never becomes less painful for a dancer – each day when she presses her head closer and closer to the ground, her thigh muscles acquiesce painfully, as she holds herself there for 15 seconds, 30 seconds, maybe even two minutes. And, should the day come when she can lay her forehead on the floor with her hips and rear end planted firmly on the ground, it will not hurt less. Do not think it will hurt less.

She will still have to breathe and count the beats and wait to feel the slight release that makes it all bearable and then resist the urge to say 'enough' and get up. Every day.

In the same way, loving never becomes any easier for the lover. There are always new risks to take, new wounds to inflict or have inflicted, and new fears to confront. However, just as the stretch becomes longer, so does the love become deeper. There is always another level of profundity waiting, with its own hazards and pitfalls, to be explored, understood and then passed.

Only recently has life taken the time to rid me of the illusion that belief is any different. It is not. It is a faculty that has to be re-exercised, reaffirmed, every day if it is not going to be lost. It is not as though, if you believe for long enough, the answers to questions, or the solutions to the contradictions, present themselves evermore willingly.

I used to think there came a point in time, in life, somewhere in the magical land of adulthood, when the universe settled; when all the questions, struggles and conflicts landed neatly in place and stayed there to form the landscape one would negotiate for the rest of one's life. What I've realized, to my disappointment, is that the world shifts and it never stops shifting. Each time we blink, or angle our gaze just a fraction differently, the sands slide and alter the terrain we thought we knew and we're forced to reconsider the magnificent plan that we spent all of high school, college and every moment up till now forming.

What does it mean to be a Bahá'í? Give me your best shot. The foremost answer, the one you might give to a seeker, probably goes something like this:

> To be a Bahá'í means you accept Bahá'u'lláh as the most recent Manifestation of God on this planet and you have committed to doing your darnedest to follow His laws and exemplify His teachings.

Nice that. A concise little package of religious belief that conveys all the pertinent information. Or, if you prefer a more abstract answer, one that addresses the *spirit* of the Faith, as opposed to its practicalities, you can just quote from our own Exemplar, 'Abdu'l-Bahá:

> Be trustworthy, sincere, affectionate and replete with chastity. Be illumined, be spiritual, be divine, be glorious, be quickened of God, be a Bahá'í. ('Abdu'l-Bahá, *Promulgation*, p. 453)

But what does it mean, really? Not the definition but the implications of belonging, to any religion really, but this one in particular. To believe, to have faith, requires that one enter a spiritual, intellectual and emotional labyrinth; and what I want to know is how, and if, you arrive at the other side. Into the light.

I struggle perpetually with this and continue to find myself drawing the same conclusions over and over again. I believe in oneness. I believe that there is a Reality, divine in design, that we, and all of existence, known and unknown, are part of. And that Reality is overseen and energized by a Supreme Being, connected to us, but complete in and of itself. The Bahá'í Faith, with its emphasis on unity, supports this idea. And yet, if this is the case, why is the Baháʼí Faith, as a religion, as a structure to which you do or do not belong, important? If we're all part and parcel of the same stock, why does it matter what you call yourself? Does that not, in fact, create division – the very thing that we are trying to work against? Is it that everyone is connected to the divine but the Baháʼís are more connected than others? That seems neither fair nor just and it's a frankly repugnant idea. Furthermore, lending divine authority to a doctrine, while useful, also gives rise to extremely painful, and unclear, dilemmas of personal sovereignty, as well as ends and means.

Education, for example, has always been, frequently ignominiously, tied to religion. How can a religious school teach a child to be an independent and critical thinker, when they also have an absolute they're trying to uphold? Yes, student, you may question and ponder and wonder but only if, in the end, you see the Truth and adhere to it. And if you don't come to it, then whatever conclusions you have drawn are false and quite probably sinful and ungodly. Any questions?

It also gives rise to an interesting, and difficult, ends versus means conundrum. If *what* you're teaching is the Absolute Truth, and unquestionably of benefit to the pupils' souls, *how* you teach it becomes a secondary question, since their souls are approaching God through the material anyway. As an educator I find this a troublesome situation and I feel history only proves my worst fears. Catholic school is notorious for its boring and hypocritical methodology. But, who cares, since once they learn the Hail Mary, they'll go to heaven anyway? I worry that Baháʼí education too easily, though unconsciously, adopts this attitude. It doesn't matter if children's class teachers are actually good teachers, if they excite and stimulate the curiosity and creativity of the students. What matters is that they've been trained in Ruhi book 3, can sing songs about Baháʼí principles and teach the youngsters to memorize quotations. Particularly in areas where Baháʼís enter communities they are not a part of in order to offer this service, I feel a sense of unease at the missionary tones of the situation.

What is more valuable? A child learning secular, science lessons but in a manner which increases his understanding and perception of the world? Or a child learning a prayer, simply by rote, getting a sticker and then going on his merry way? What has increased his ability to function as a creative, aware, active member of society? Granted, this is not an either-or situation. It is entirely possible for religion to be taught in a meaningful way and science to be taught badly but I do not think that, with regard to religious education, we can shrug off the means simply because the end is God.

Sex is another deeply troubling area for religion. I want to be very clear here – I understand and support the Bahá'í principles on sexuality and I do not think that they, inherently, create unhealthy sexual dynamics. Indeed, I feel precisely the opposite – I think that defining our fundamental nature outside of our gender is the very salvation of that most delightful and sacred act. However, it is the manner in which we approach our sexuality, pre-marriage, that is extremely troubling. What Bahá'í youth are taught regarding sex can be summed up as follows: Sex is fine but only once you're married. Now, go play Scrabble.

The difficulty here is that we live in a highly sexualized society and one that gives deeply penetrating, and conflicting, ideas regarding sexuality. First and foremost, sex, violence and power are all deeply interrelated. A woman holds power when she is desired sexually by a man and a man proves his power by conquering a woman sexually, sometimes violently. Because we aren't supposed to be engaging in sexual acts until we're married, this discussion never enters Bahá'í discourse on sexuality. Which is a shame, because in our personal relationships, and even in our fantasies, we play out the unhealthy power dynamics we see around us with no counterweight or vocabulary. We are not neutral beings who suddenly discover our genitalia, and all its implications, the day a wedding ring gets put on our finger. We are sponges, absorbing from infancy the extremely powerful messages regarding man and womanhood, and our law of chastity is only the germ of a counterbalance.

Furthermore, should a Bahá'í have a sexual relationship outside of marriage, there are no guidelines on how to understand and control the intense forces unleashed with physical intimacy.

I do not understand what we are supposed to do. Are we to circumvent entirely the discussion on healthy sexual identity and interaction, because we do not sanction it outside of marriage, leaving the Baháʼí youth to discover, through their own numerous, painful mistakes, how to manage themselves as gendered beings? That seems incredibly puritanical and unfair to me. But, then, is it acceptable to discuss sexuality outside of marriage, in a fair and reasonable light (not simply that it is sinful and destructive) although we do not believe it is permissible?

It's important here to understand that I am not merely talking about intercourse or any sexual *act* for that matter. I'm talking about addressing mentalities, the relationship between sexual attractiveness and self-worth so entrenched for young women and the tendency to objectify and conquer those women that we see manifested in men. And then, how these detrimental perceptions are played out within relationships, in ways that deny both genders their nobility and subjectivity as spiritual and sexual beings. Our nifty little concept of the equality between men and women does not immunize us against sexism in any of its various and pernicious forms. Nor can we isolate sex from the intellect or culture, and it seems to me that some manner of frank dialogue or critical framework would do much to support the Baháʼí goal of wholesome and stable marriage.

Art, also, has frequently found itself in confrontation with religion and religious sensibilities. As a Baháʼí I have a duty to my religion to try and embody the principles of my Faith. But as an artist I also have a responsibility to my craft to create significant, powerful works and to represent my experience truthfully. Although these two mandates are by no means mutually exclusive, they can very easily come into conflict with each other. What if I want to make a piece that is possibly offensive or painful? What if I want to use curse words or obscene images? Because perhaps I am feeling rage or surrounded by obscenity and I have a need to process and express my reactions to these things. What do I do? Now, we can discuss at length motivation or intent but those are individual questions and I am addressing art as it relates to the Baháʼí Faith as a structure. So, could I make such an incendiary piece, even though I'm a Bahá'í? It might shock or offend but is that a sin? As a Bahá'í, can I only express the sweetness of life, those times that are so often meaningless without the salt, the bitter, bitter, salt, to savour? Or, I could make it and then turn it against a wall, burn the poem. But art is communicative by nature and one half of its definition is that it is shared with others, perhaps reaching across our so frequent isolation to give someone a sense of commonality – the relief that they are not alone.

There are catchwords in our religion that are frequently used to assuage these tremblings – moderation, purity of motive, wisdom, consultation – but too often these terms gloss over the raw, frightening, issue: in order to be a Bahá'í, do I have to deny myself my own expression? Self-denial, in a sense, is present in all religions and is a perfectly acceptable doctrine. But on which side does this particular matter land? The puritanical or the reasonable?

The Bahá'í Faith itself teaches that we are both angelic and diabolic. 'Each child is potentially the light of the world – and at the same time its darkness,' says 'Abdu'l-Bahá. ('Abdu'l-Bahá, *Selections*, p. 130) The whole purpose of existence is to struggle and, in the struggle, bring forth our own divinity. And if that's the case, any artist in search of truth and universal communication would be no more than a court jester if she only expressed the light. To deny or negate the struggle is to negate our purpose and we end up with only meaningless platitudes that belong on greeting cards and do nothing to quicken the human experience.

My life is not a triumph, peppered from time to time, for excitement, with metaphysical conundrums. It is one long struggle whose triumphs are small and quotidian. I forgave one tiny betrayal or I listened without judgement. I gave up a seat, though tired, or I reflected, briefly, someone's dignity so they could know it. I did not take the last or biggest one.

I do not think, for one moment, that these 'good deeds' or 'charitable works' add up to anything. I will not receive a grand tally on my deathbed. It is only in relinquishing the gripping need for it all to Amount To Something that I am able to give freely. Keeping score only reveals the deep indebtedness we have to each other and, moreover, to God. It is a balance that could never be settled. And it will never be easy, or even easier, but there will be, one day at a time, moments of redemption to which we deprive or avail ourselves.

After all this, after all these railings and rantings and pounding my head against the theology I love, I come back, daily, to the same choice: to be or not to be. The simple decision to knock this all down a notch, to toss this religion in with 'universal wisdom' and then select whatever is most personally meaningful would resolve much of my existential angst. I would no longer experience the panic and stomach wrenching paralysis that occurs whenever I Can't Answer Something, whenever the rift between my personal and intellectual experience and the teachings of my religion becomes, seemingly, unbridgeable. I could throw in the towel, walk out the way one does on an uncompromising lover, wash my hands of the mandate to comprehend and articulate creation, cosmology and human destiny. To just be done with it. Perhaps I would sleep peacefully then and finally be able to discuss the human spirit tranquilly, over a cup of tea, comment from a neutral observer's perspective, instead of someone fighting tooth and nail with the universe while her immortal soul hangs in the balance.

I admit, this attracts me. But this would not answer my queries. It would simply remove them, the way a dictator does a troublesome minority. No, I have knocked and the door has opened and only a coward would take fright of the rustlings in the dark, turn heel because the light is not flooding the entranceway. I have entered and now I will eat up the darkness with my questions. The thread in this maze is my own voice, conversing with the Unknown and the divine. God brought creation into existence with the word. And now I will call His work into the light with mine.

Epilogue

Dear Dad,

Does this frighten or disturb you? Do you recognize in these difficult, frustrated words, your daughter? The child who is partially you and who you should know, in some sense, as yourself; the nature and the predispositions, as well as all the years of careful, so very careful, nurturing. You have put yourself in, your sperm first (that was the easy part), then your time, your own fears, your labour, your knowledge, practical and mundane, historical and social. I learned how to ride a bike from you, I learned about Lenin and Stalin and Trotsky with his unfortunate icepick. I learned about Bob Dylan, Diana Ross and how to listen. How to weigh situations and make decisions with care. Play backgammon, cook and laugh heartily. With all this input, is this output surprising, unsettling or strange?

This is perhaps where your daughter, your youngest child, ends and a human being, as unknown as any other, begins. Because these are existence questions, universal most likely in structure but also particular in content, borne from my life, my own 20 years on this planet, as I have lived it. But you have lived those 20 years with me and so you can see that these difficulties are not coming out of nowhere. They are coming, in part, from you. And I do not mean that in any blameworthy sense. Simply that you tilled, arduously and lovingly, the soil from which I have sprung. Is this the plant, the 'tree of life', that you were expecting?

I have wanted to write you countless times, express and perhaps put to rest, the tail-swallowing questions that chase themselves around in my head. Straighten them out in the written word, lay them head to tail on the line and offer them to you to discern. To see if, from your altitude of experience, you could distinguish some sort of pattern, or direction, could tell me where this is all going, reassure me that it is in fact going somewhere. Somewhere you maybe have been and that I will arrive with my beliefs intact.

I'm writing this in an airport, sitting in the hot sunlight with children shouting and ricocheting all around, and it is embarrassing, and somewhat inexplicable, but I have begun to cry.

Some Poems by Anisa Qualls

This is What it Means to be Religious

These choices
these choices

these choices.
So bitter to me.
Cheers
to this caustic draft,
let's drain it down
to the dregs.
Nothing else fills me
or quenches my thirst
so I lie here
panting
licking
sweat instead.
This brew
so potent
so horribly pungent
promises salvation
in annihilation.
The elixir of existence
demands all that it guarantees:
accept death
and you will receive life.
How can I choose
between
immortal solitude
and eternal thirst?
Staring
at the sour
choking potion
I curse the Winemaker,
and drink.

Who Eats the Oranges?

I dreamt about you last night.
Your high open windows
the smell of roses
and the warm scratchiness of the carpet
against my shins

all speaking directly
to my only real truth:
the need for nearness
that resonates off my ribs,
circulates through my blood
and changes
the way I see.
I dreamt about
the time and distance,
the ship that leaves
the shoreline in the horizon
the sand pouring so swiftly
through the hourglass,
marking
my only real fear:
the possibility of separation.
Home ceased to be a place for me
long ago,
until I sat within your walls
simultaneously wondering
who eats the oranges
and seeking my salvation
and there was no distance between the two.
No seeping wound,
the breach generated
when creation and Creator
are severed,
separated into me and Thee
light and sun
water and wetness.
Sitting within you,
every piece
just different forms of dust
reaching for sunlight
and I was finally still enough
to hear things grow.

Lunar Eclipse in Harlem

The world is awake with me tonight.
Rilke and Bahá'u'lláh
and the black boy on the subway
who can't keep his music to himself
and Sherman Alexie and Bessie Head.
They all have things to tell me tonight.

The world is alive with me tonight.
It's careening through these subway tunnels
arising in skyscrapers
singing in sirens
and pushing out of Manhattan
over the Atlantic

way past both poles
and through the milky way
extending itself in an enormous pubescence.

The world is thrusting its pelvis tonight
and I can only try and ride its rhythm.
Hope my heart
can keep up with this beat
that is reverberating through the globe,
putting us all off balance
and making everyone stop
so they can notice
that they're walking on miracles.
Stop and feel their stories
our stories
that are shaking
quaking up from the ground
where they've been too long buried.
Up and through their legs
making us all shudder
with the truth of ourselves

and the incredible echo of the Divine
that has been humming, buzzing
and waiting
for so long to be heard.
No friends, that was not just static.
That was the celestial orchestra tuning up
trying to get us all in key
and now
they are ready to play.

Forget Howard Stern –
I am the ultimate shock jock:
Telling people
that Christ has actually already returned three times
and that their bodies
are the temples of the kingdom of God
on earth,
so they should take care of them already.
Not treat them like dens of iniquity
and pits of heresy.
Who is there for me to make love to
who will understand this,
and see in each kiss
an act of creation
a salutation
to the living of life
and open my legs
the way the sun opens a flower:
moved by the desire
not to take
or even to give
but to add a tiny movement

to the symphony of Infinity
and so become part of it.
And because there is no one
I cook whenever I can

and laugh as loudly as possible,
producing at all times
the tiny threads
that allow me to be stretched
across an angel's violin,
lie taut
on a timeless cello.
Which is why I'm vibrating
with the world tonight
because we are all being plucked
and yanked
and jangled
in the hopes
that we are finally in tune,
well-rehearsed
and ready
to give the concert
of a universal lifetime.

Water Birth (for Millard Qualls)

In many ways
it is like waiting
for a birth:
I keep my cell phone on all the time,
the late night calls
that update me
on the condition.
It would seem that the water has broken
and it is only a matter of time now
which is all life really is, anyway.
The universe has dilated its first centimetres,
opening.
Grandpa,
can you see the light?

The mother and daughter I live with
are fighting again

and their bitterness just seems small and sad
after our conversation,
in which I heard contractions,
and it became clear
that loving words
are the only ones worth saying.

We are all with you, Grandpa
standing on this shore together.
With eternity lapping at our feet,

this is the closest any of us
have ever come
to going home.

We are all looking out
on these golden depths together,
feeling humbled and blessed
as we taste grace
like salt, in the air.
This truly
is the final frontier
and the tide is coming forward
to carry you home.

I am currently in a country
that has no coast.
A land confined,
there is no place where we can see forever
stretching beyond
our finite selves.
No vision to lift us
above
the human condition
and we are all
the worse for it.

So go then, Grandfather,
take this chance at limitlessness
and leave the burden of your body
to us.
We will bear it solemnly
while you are born
to the surging sea.

Matthew Morrissey

Matt Morrissey, who was 20 at the time of writing, was born and raised in Scotland. He was raised in a Bahá'í family, has one brother and is an active member of the Scottish Bahá'í community.

Sacrifice

Her name was Amber. Her eyes were of the deepest blue. Her hair was dark, glinting red in the sun. Her smile could melt the coldest of hearts. Her generosity knew no bounds. I still remember the first time I met her. Stunned by her beauty, I spent hours mustering up the courage to speak to her. I'm definitely not shy but when it comes to the opposite sex it's so hard. What to say? What to do? Are you gonna run the risk of looking stupid and crack a joke? Somehow I managed it. We met the next day for coffee. Her glowing face was matched by her personality.

After a few more weeks we became an item. I couldn't believe how lucky I was. Sure she was cute, yet so kind, so caring and even 'got' my twisted sense of humour. And best of all, with me being a Bahá'í, she didn't seem to mind that I didn't want to express my feelings through sex. That's always the hardest bit. Countless are the times I've met nice girls, seen them for a few weeks and then it gets to that awkward 'are you gonna stay over tonight' moment. It's harsh, very harsh. I mean, I'm a human being. I have desires and it's hard to say no when you want something, something that I've been told is the greatest thing on earth. No matter what, the old 'I really like you but I don't wanna do that' line never works. Then you end up *'friends'*, which really means you pretend to be civil but never talk to each other again. For once, though, this wasn't an issue. Maybe this time I was onto something good?

The weeks rolled into months that rolled into years. I couldn't have been happier. How could I be happier? I had a loving family, great friends, a nice apartment and the jewel in my crown: I had Amber. We laughed, we shared, we even sometimes cried. It was actually like a cheesy chick flick. Walks in the parks, romantic dinners, nights out, watching movies. Even my parents liked her. Things couldn't get better, in my eyes.

Slowly, dark clouds began to creep behind those big blue eyes. Depression began to take hold in her. No matter what I tried, nothing seemed able to stop winter taking hold in her heart. Eventually I noticed red scrapes on her arms. They were self-inflicted. I prayed for her. I did everything I could to make her life easier. I managed to convince her to see a therapist. It's so hard to see someone you love so miserable. Yes, by this time I loved her and she loved me.

Slowly things seemed to be getting better. She was happier. She was getting her work done. The anti-depressants and counselling were helping. But it was not to be. One grim night the floodgates opened. Amongst problems of homesickness and losing friends, it seemed that my Faith was one of the causes. I never tried to force the Faith on her but she knew quite a bit about it. 'I love you', she said, 'but I never want to get married. Ever. To anyone. I don't see the point in it. If two people love each other, isn't that enough? I still want to be with you and spend the rest of my life with you.'

Nothing could ever have prepared me for that moment. It was like taking a gun to my head and painting the walls with my blood. Like ripping my heart out in front of me. No physical pain could ever compare. How could someone I love so much think this way? How could we ever go on if this was the way she felt? No, we could not continue like this. Slowly, emotion left my face as I realized that there was no future with her. My dreams of happiness with her had collapsed. Words cannot describe that feeling, one I'd never wish on anyone.

'If we ever had children I wouldn't want them to be Bahá'í.' I think she was counting on immaculate conception for that one. Like I said earlier, I have a twisted sense of humour. As the old proverb goes, this was rubbing salt in my wounds. It had never even occurred to me that my children would not be raised in the knowledge of the Faith. I could never live with myself if I deprived my own flesh and blood of that which I treasure most. At many times it's all I have. I couldn't let my future children grow up without the influence of Bahá'u'lláh.

I pleaded with her. I strove so hard to make her understand, to explain the Bahá'í concepts of marriage, to show that Bahá'í parents bring their children up with Bahá'í morals and with clear knowledge of the Faith but never force it on them. But nothing got through. Her mind was made up. I went home afterwards and cried. I cried more than I can remember. Although I'm not afraid to show my feminine side, this was torturous. There was no hope for us. I had to end it. There was no way I could abandon the Faith to be with her. Things always change. Friends and girlfriends come and go. Sometimes people even die. But the Faith is constant. It is always with you, guiding you through the good and the bad. It picks you up off the ground when you cannot. It makes life meaningful. I'd tasted life without it before and there's nothing there. Much as I loved her, I couldn't live without it.

The 'breaking up' conversation was the worst I've ever had, with anyone, ever. It's bad enough having your own heart broken, but it's another thing to then have to break the heart of your beloved. What was said will stay between us. Let's just say she didn't make it easy on me.

Afterwards, once again I cried and prayed. I felt so wretched, so guilty that I'd inflicted so much pain on one I held so dear. But I had no choice. It was the right thing to do. I didn't want to lose her, I really didn't, but I had to let her go. For starters, we could never be the same again after that night. It would be like fire and ice trying to live together. Also, I didn't want to end up like so many of my friends; stuck in unhealthy relationships that were going nowhere for years and years. Looking back I know I made the right choice. I hope she finds the peace she deserves.

It would be easy to look at this experience as negative. Sure, it was extremely painful and leaving her was the hardest thing I've ever done but I feel that I've only gained through it. I know now exactly what I'm looking for in a girlfriend, what I want and what I don't. More importantly, I've learned that I can actually love another human being more than I ever imagined. I can put someone else before myself, although not at the expense of my own health. I've also found out a lot about myself and who I am. I am a Bahá'í.

I've always been but never felt it so much as now. I love my Faith so much and I could never part with it, not for anything. Most importantly, I learned what sacrifice is. I've always been a bit superficial about sacrifices before, like, 'Oh, look at me! I'm sacrificing by going to feast instead of a party – I'm so spiritual.' Well, I guess that is a very minor sacrifice. But true sacrifice is very painful. And it's always something you really don't want to lose. I didn't want to lose her. I missed her for so long afterwards. I still think of her. Yet in that strange paradoxical way things seem to happen in our Faith, letting go benefited me in more ways than I could imagine. Almost six months on I can look back without anger and with minimal sorrow and realize that in some strange way I was blessed with this. I've grown stronger through it all. My reason for writing this is not for sympathy but to share my experience with any other Bahá'ís who I'm sure may have or may be going through the same type of thing. Hopefully my story will help.

Tahirih Alia

Born in 1981, Tahirih Alia grew up in a Bahá'í family in Arizona. A graduate of Maxwell International Bahá'í School, class of '99, she holds an undergraduate degree from the University of Arizona and wrote her contribution from her post in Guatemala, where she was working as a witness to the testimony of indigenous peoples regarding acts of genocide. She recently graduated from the London School of Economics with a Master's degree in Human Rights (2006).

I'm just finishing my first full week of 'accompaniment' here in Guatemala, after two long months of preparation. I could never have imagined it to be so beautiful.

I'm living in a legal human rights office in a small pueblo, Rabinal, and then hiking several miles up into the mountains each day to visit families who are witnesses in the genocide cases. It is so many experiences at once: the physical beauty of the country is more than I can possibly describe; the opportunity to see a way of living that is entirely different and intensely beautiful; and, more than anything, finding myself relating to, understanding and admiring people with whom one would think I could have nothing in common. It's been a good lesson in 'the oneness of humanity', to recognize that we are, really, the same inside, and a profound realization of the power of the human spirit. I had started to realize this when I was working at the Children's Shelter, spending hours laughing and playing and caring for children who had next to nothing, abandoned by their families. Now, looking in the bright, shining faces of the Maya-Ach'i, it is so difficult to imagine that they witnessed the most horrible violence that could be inflicted upon a people. This kind of resiliency totally floors me and seeing the way that these brave souls have moved on and pushed forward when I'm sure I would have given up has really helped me to process my own traumas and tragedies. Anyway, I've also been keeping in close touch with my spirit.

The contour of my day very much resembles that of this country – mountainous, severe, tragic, beautiful. Amidst the heat and the dust and the onslaught of various thoughts and emotions, I quietly excuse myself and go to wash my hands and face. I find a quiet place and turn to the east to say my obligatory noonday prayer. In this moment, all of the traffic of living is set in pause as I retreat into the space where I exist only in relation to that which is divine. This, surely, will be the most important part of my day.

To ask what it is that keeps me connected to the Bahá'í Faith is like asking what keeps my heart beating, my lungs breathing, my feet moving. To be honest, I am not entirely certain, but I am aware that it is essential to my continued existence and that it is inseparable from who I am at my core.

A WARM PLACE IN MY HEART

I spent a great deal of time in my adolescence evading and avoiding my spiritual commitment to Bahá'u'lláh. It took years of running and hiding to realize that the commitment, that divine connection, existed inside of me all along. As much as I was a woman, that my name was Tahirih or any other fundamental facet of my being, it became clear that I was a Bahá'í and that this had been true for as long as I had been alive. It was my first duty to recognize this.

The second duty has been to live in that reality, a process profoundly more complicated, painful, beautiful and transformative than the initial realization itself. The implication is that I live in a state of constant interplay and relationship with my Faith. It is the rock that grounds me, the single constant amidst perpetual change. It is my greatest inspiration, providing hope and courage in moments of weakness. It is my greatest challenge, calling me to a standard of which I seem to fall short time and again.

My most recent struggle, in which I am still engaged, has been to reconcile my academic and political convictions with my spiritual beliefs. For a long while I have compartmentalized them in entirely separate spheres and have even found them at odds with one another. As I uncover the layers of this Faith, however, I am amazed to find a radical message that speaks directly to the exigencies of this time. It is not a passive message but one calling us all to devote ourselves to social change, to work endlessly to bring justice to the world and to defend the victims of oppression.

So it is that I find my Faith stretching out over the entire arch of my self identity, from the most intensely personal relationship in my life to the public expression of everything I believe about the world I live in.

And far more than all of this, my Faith is maintained by an indescribably intangible, truly mystical experience that has graciously painted my life with the most vibrant of colours. In the piercing note of a violin, in a vibrant Arizona sunset, in the cloud forests of Guatemala, I feel the divine presence resonating within me and all around me. For this, I am a Bahá'í.

July 2005

With just over one month left of my time here in Guatemala, I am amazed at just how quickly time passes. I feel the pressing need to take it all in and I urge my heart to remember the landscapes, faces, sounds and smells and allow them to change me with their beauty.

There are so many words that need to be said about this world in which we live and the crises of war – not just wars fought between nation states but all of the millions of wars of people oppressing other people through economics, sexism, racism and one thousand other mechanisms.

We need actions to give life to our words. We need to conjure up all of the creativity dwelling inside of our collective unconscious to dream up new visions of reality and set to work building our new world governed by the laws of equality and oneness rather than borders and profit margins. I feel like I am just waking up.

Today I will send you some of my thoughts on the world around me, in the hope that we can conspire together and find new ways to defy the insane logic of an unjust system with reverence and mischief, and imagine new ways to usher in a dynamic and spiritual revolution.

The Market

It's just past 5 a.m. on Sunday morning when the giant truck, crammed tightly with passengers, comes barrelling down the mountain. The vehicle pauses just long enough for us to board and a strong, calloused hand reaches down to help me up.

As we situate ourselves in the overcrowded truck bed, we exchange friendly greetings with our fellow passengers. Many of them carry huge baskets loaded with tomatoes, bananas, mangoes and avocados. We are on our way back to Rabinal, where every Sunday the town's centre fills with people from surrounding villages selling their goods in the open stalls of the town's market.

Many of these people are the same folks that I have the pleasure of visiting each week. They have walked me through their cornfields and excitedly explained community projects in organic agriculture. I have played with their children and shared meals of black beans and tortillas in crowded, one-room adobe homes. They've lovingly offered suggestions and treatments for the various scrapes, sunburns and ailments I've acquired in my time here. They have told their stories of the violence, of hiding in the mountains without food or shelter for years, evading the military soldiers.

The last several months have been a blessing; how often my heart has ached at all the beauty and wonder around me. Just days ago I was sitting on a dirt porch, enjoying the fresh afternoon breeze while visiting a family, talking about our different cultures. The mother looked up and said, 'We look different from one another. My skin is a different colour from yours. But our blood, our hearts, are the same. We are a family. We are family.'

It is this sentiment that informs my perception of the world – that we are one and that we are charged with the duty and the honour to serve and protect one another.

The Colonial Legacy

I am sitting high above the dusty streets of Rabinal on a mountaintop they call 'Cayup'. Here I find the crumbling ruins of what was the capital city of this region hundreds of years ago. This site was once the heart of Maya-Ach'i civilization, before the Spanish colonizers arrived and forced the indigenous people from the mountains into the valley, where their forced labour would contribute to one of the greatest transfers of wealth in human history.

I wonder what all of it means. If genocide is the effort to exterminate, in whole or in part, a racial/ethnic group, I ask myself: when, exactly, did the genocide in Guatemala begin and when will it end? Are a people, long pushed against a wall, suddenly being pushed over it? If so, what will we do to stop it?

Our Responses

Back in Rabinal, I am having dinner with friends when I hear news of the bombings in London. It is yet another in the series of acts of terrorism directed at the powerful western ideology and policy embodied in the G8, WTO and other such global entities.

I feel my heart drop into my stomach. My spirit wilts in defeat. How can it be? ...

Who are we if we resort to the use of violence to fight a violent system? If we use the tactics of the oppressors, how can we claim to be any better? How can we create something that is new by using old, ineffective methods? And what will be left of this precious, fragile world if guns and bombs are the tools we use for conflict resolution?

Perhaps the most challenging aspect of non-violence is insisting upon the humanity of our opposition. We must recognize the full horror of racism or capitalism or terrorism while maintaining that the opponent is a member of our own family. This does not mean that criminals deserve impunity but that we refuse to destroy them with violence. It means drawing a line between justice and vengeance. The true revolutionary knows that the goal is deep change, not the settling of old scores.

Unfortunately, the path of non-violence ensures that those who are oppressed and suffering will have to suffer more without relief. But this is the sacrifice that is to be made in the path of genuine transformation.

> Where your opposition has expected anger and hatred, you offer love. Where the opposition insists on seeing you as an object, you insist on treating the opposition as consisting of unique individuals who merit compassion. In short, we can change the terms of the struggle, can transform it – and in the process, while we must often 'unjustly suffer', out of that comes the hope of justice. There is no justice in history except as we create it. And the creation of justice demands we accept a large part of the pain of conflict and change. Why would we do this? Because, by the grace of God or accident, we have stumbled on a truth which has taught us that our opposition is our brother, our sister, and we will pay a very high price, if necessary, before inflicting the pain on others which history has inflicted on us. Our goal is transformation and reconciliation, and that is what a revolution is about. (McReynolds, in *Philosophy of Nonviolence*)

'Maltyox' (Thank You)

I do not know how to say the words in a way that will let you hear the gratitude resonating in my spirit. Thank you. Your letters of support and encouragement have pushed me forward when my feet were tired. So many of you have engaged with me in meaningful dialogue, asking challenging questions and offering thoughtful responses. Thank you for your bold hearts and your commitment to change.

October 2005

London is beautiful and exciting and there is so much happening, it is completely impossible for me to take part in all the things that call out to me.

The programme is a MSc in Human Rights, at the LSE, and it's rigorous and wonderful and all those things, you know . . . I'm taking a core course in the key foundations and issues in human rights, a course on the politics of reconciliation and another on complex emergencies.

It is, truly, what my heart has been wanting to study for a few years now and so I am happy in that regard. But the material is heavy, dealing with genocide and justice, famine, war and peace . . . there are no simple answers and the nature of the school and the programme force me to question every instinct and assumption I've ever had – this is learning, I know, but it's exhausting as well.

I'm in the middle of a really intense paper on the Rwandan genocide . . .

May 2006

Britain. Not much to say. I'm not actually that aware that I'm in 'Britain' but very much that I'm in 'London'. The whole 'global city'. It was really hard at first, coming from Guatemala. There was a lot of culture shock and adjustment. The first term was hard, hard . . . emotionally, mentally, ethically. But you get used to things, I guess.

July 2006

These days are full of beauty and sadness and joy...

I just got back from three amazing weeks in Colombia. I'm doing research right now for my thesis, which I thought was going to be on 'Grassroots Level Peace Initiatives' but I tried to just listen to people while I was down there in that beautiful mystery and my new title is 'The Political Economy of Forced Displacement and Strategies of Resistance'. I'm really excited about it.

Colombia has the highest level of forced displacement in the world and the effects of this phenomenon are devastating. Being internally displaced means that you lose the capacity to provide your own food, shelter and so on. And when you are an internally displaced person (meaning, not an international refugee) this situation is even worse because the international provisions for refugees (which are themselves insufficient) do not apply to you. Poverty, alcoholism, prostitution and hunger are some of the words that come to mind when I think about the situation affecting these people (and there are, literally, millions of them).

So for my dissertation I'm going to try and look at some of the causes of this phenomenon, both the political and the economic. But I'm also intent on focusing on the way that people *resist* with their bodies and their actions and their words and refuse to be displaced.

I spent a couple of weeks hanging out in San Jose de Apartado, which is a 'peace community' in resistance. While I was there one of the community leaders received a really brutal death threat and the community decided that it would be best if he went into retreat while they decided what to do. So I went on a long trek into the jungle with him and a few other community members. We spent several days in an abandoned house, fished in the river and ate fresh corn. It was so beautiful and such an honour to spend time with some of the most dynamic and brilliant people I've ever met. And also frustrating and heartbreaking, given the context of our journey.

He returned to the community and things are going on as they do: communal work-groups and heat and rain and living...

He said to me when I was leaving (I was really worried about his safety) that he is sure that he will be killed eventually. But, he said, the alternative is to submit to the violence and live in terror and fear and flee the community. A fate more terrible than death, they say . . .

Back in the capital I had the pleasure of hanging out with an anarchist collective called 'Creaccion Espacios', which is doing really wonderful work. I fell in love a thousand times and made friends that I hope will be for life.

I'm back in London town again, relishing the long, long summer days and the flat is full of friends and food and music. It doesn't get much better than this, I'm thinking . . .

But the joy of friendship and playing is tempered (it always is, isn't it?) by worries that clamour around inside of me. My parents are in Haifa at the moment and I'm scheduled to be there this Friday to meet them. The recent bombings make me preoccupied for the safety of my family, which is compounded by being deeply concerned for the safety of families on both sides of the border. The convergence is one that brings my ongoing spiritual–political dilemma to its most heightened pitch. I'm tryin' real hard to stay calm and just let myself be guided by Truth but then I called my grandma just now and she's a total mess, worried and watching the news religiously. She started telling me about bomb shelters in Haifa and the fires in California and I couldn't help but be overcome, momentarily, by a kind of apocalyptic, doom-like feeling.

So now I'm writing this email to people that I love. And remembering that beauty is everywhere. And there is much to be grateful for, as always.

Marzieh Thorne

Marzieh Lorna Thorne was 16 when her mother shared the following selections from her youthful reflections. Marzieh lives in Sacramento, California. She was adopted at birth by Gayle Hoover

Thorne and Douglass Thorne. Her interests include her black Lab, Middy, being independent, working and having freedom.

Reports
1 February 2002

This is an assignment from Mrs Brown: to look up the word 'racist' and give a definition. I have chosen to write a little more than that.

Racist ... it is an adjective. It means to be prejudiced or to discriminate against someone because of religion, race or external, uncontrollable factor.

Sound familiar? I think so! Sometimes it happens in our classroom. In our reading class we read and you, as the teacher, take attendance: Marzieh, Carrie, Raquelle, Gurdkhi. We hear 'Ha, Ha, Ha!' For some reason that's so funny. Many kids make fun of his name; kids like Nick, Estaven, Steven, Caeser, Josh and sometimes Carlos and Jamar. Just because he comes from another country and has a different language, which means he has a different kind of name, he is teased all the time and it's not fair to him or anyone who has to hear it.

Racism is a big thing for my family. We don't like it! We have many races in our family. Our friends are Chinese, Indian, Pakistani, black, white and more. My religion says that racism and sexism are twin evils. They must be continuously battled against in our individual, private lives and collectively. Racism is not only harmful to the victim; it also corrupts and poisons the soul of the perpetrator and the social structures that allow it to be institutionalized.

So it's everyone's responsibility to stick up for the weak, the one being teased. Whether they are of a different race or religion or disabled, overweight, whatever. We are all just as guilty for letting it keep happening. This is why I get so mad and want this to stop because it's not right and for you, as the teacher, to ignore it is even worse. I don't know if you ignore it because you don't care or you just don't know what to do about it. But I know that you know it's happening! This is why I have now involved the principal to help bring it to an end.

Sincerely,
Marzieh Thorne, age 12

A WARM PLACE IN MY HEART

Bosch Bahá'í School Journal
Summer 2002

My mother drove me to Burlingame, California, so that I could ride down to Bosch with my friends Roya, Amanda and Malika. We arrived there on Saturday, 17 August 2002. It was my fifth summer here. It was great fun. At first I got registered. Then I went to find my cabin. After I got unpacked and got my stuff arranged in my cabin, we all went down to Martha Root Hall, which is a big room with chairs where people meet and talk.

They told us what we'd be doing for the week. It sounded great. After our meeting, which lasted for an hour, we went to dinner. After that we went up to our cabins for an hour to talk. There were six other girls besides me and our cabin leader, whose name was Shomace.

Then we went down to Martha Root Hall to read and answer questions about virtues. From that exercise I learned how to deal with other people's negative attitudes and how to avoid backbiting and negative impulses. I haven't learned this completely but I did learn how to avoid these things. Since no one is perfect, I'll never completely learn to avoid these things but I can try.

Normally after our cabin time it would be game night but this time we had to learn to be kind to each other and not make others feel bad so when we do have our games, it will be more fun and people's feelings won't get hurt. After this learning night together we went to bed.

The next five mornings we'd get up at 6:15, brush our teeth, wash our faces and go out to the grove for prayers. After that we would do one hour of service. Since the 75th anniversary of Bosch was coming up, we did a lot of gardening in the entryway and cut down weeds. Also, as fire season was coming up, we removed a lot of sticks and logs in the forest. The routine for removing the logs was to use three people, me, a boy student and my teacher Mr Behruzi. We were some of the only ones who wanted to do this hard labour.

The other kids would load up the trucks and we would drive them to another field and unload them. Every morning at this time we were able to do probably four to five loads. You might think this was really hard to do but last August in the Santa Cruz mountains it never got over 75 degrees and in the mornings when we were working so hard it was only about 52 degrees, so I had no problem of oppressive heat to deal with. I love to work but cannot do it in extreme heat, which is why I hate Sacramento summers. It was fun to have a break from that hot weather.

Following the service we'd go to breakfast, which took another hour. Every breakfast was delicious and juicy and different every time, and the same was true for the other two meals of each day. Just because we were in the forest didn't mean cooking was done over fires. Bosch has its own dining room and industrial kitchen. Other amenities include luxury bathrooms in the dining area, near the classrooms and in Martha Root Hall. There are showers and bathrooms in the cabins as well. This is not a chintzy operation. It is a wonderful getaway.

After breakfast we'd go back to our cabins, take showers and clean the cabins for the 'Cleanest Cabin' award. Then we would go back to Martha Root Hall for any of the day's necessary information, followed by class. In class we talked about the Báb (one of the two Messengers from God for the Bahá'í Faith) and the dawn-breakers (early believers). Then we'd have an hour's break and go up to the bookshop/café and read. Then we'd go up to our cabins for bunk time and talk about the events of the day or take a quick nap, then go down for lunch. We'd eat and then have 90 minutes of recreation time. We would swim in our luxury pool, play basketball or volleyball or go for hikes in the forest. We could also go back up to the café/bookshop.

Then we'd go up to our cabins again so the swimmers could shower and we'd go back down again for class, which lasted 90 minutes. This time we'd switch classrooms, going to another teacher for a change. This was followed by dinner, a 15 minute break and then we'd go back to class (our home rooms) and resume whatever we had discussed in the morning class.

After class we'd go back to our cabins to get coats for the night. We'd then go outside for about half an hour and walk around, then go back to Martha Root Hall for game night. Game night was different every time. One night was for songs, another for art quotes and then we'd do art about them. Another night was for dancing, such as the limbo and a game called 'Where the West Wind Blows'. Basically, that was the routine for each day.

During this session there were fewer youth than usual. We had about 32 kids, versus about 132 last year. Since there were fewer youth, it was easier for us to bond and make close friends. Fewer cabins were used and there was more room in the pool as well.

My friend Malika wrote this poem which shows some of what we all learned at Bosch:

> Men or women, black or white,
> We know equality's always right.
> For world peace, we must unite.
> To achieve that goal, we cannot fight.

Alexis Nieland

Raised in Haifa, Alexis Nieland is a member of the extended clan of the Perreault family of Saskatchewan, many of whom are Bahá'ís. He currently resides in Saskatchewan, where he works and is involved with the Bahá'í community.

The Perfect Encounter
Haifa, 29 May 2005

I was born and raised in Haifa, Israel, by a German father and French-Canadian mother. My parents have been serving at the Bahá'í World Centre for many years. I have therefore lived all my life in a Bahá'í environment. As you may know, people who offer to serve at the Bahá'í World Centre come from all over the world for a specific period of time. I grew up in this environment. All my life I was exposed to different cultures and ethnic diversity. I was also well aware of the religious diversity existing in Israel. I noticed that the members of the various religious and ethnic groups did not socialize together. In fact, they had very little contact with each other.

One incident which I experienced while I was doing my year of service in Haifa truly confirmed my faith in the Cause of Bahá'u'lláh. It occurred one afternoon, while I was waiting with a group of youth to catch a sherut (Israeli taxi) to go to Bahjí. After some time, a sherut driver pulled up and we climbed in. The taxi driver turned to us and immediately said, 'You must be Bahá'ís.' We responded, 'Yes, how did you know?' He replied, 'Most people here, except for the Bahá'ís, rarely socialize with people who differ from their own culture, race and religion. They have a strong tendency to stay with the people who share the same traditions, beliefs and ethnicity; however, the Bahá'ís seem to be happy to be with all people.'

This comment from the taxi driver confirmed in me the true meaning of the teachings of our beloved Cause. I am proud to say that I am a Bahá'í because as Bahá'ís we are striving for the advancement of mankind.

> If the inhabitants of a great continent become one spirit in different bodies marvellous progress will be made and if the people of the entire globe are welded into one great commonwealth the prayer, 'Thy kingdom come, Thy will be done on earth as in heaven', will be a reality for each will have the kingdom within himself. ('Abdu'l-Bahá, *Divine Philosophy*, p. 184)

In my efforts to serve the Faith I wish to work towards establishing this Kingdom on Earth. I feel that this may be achieved only through the teachings of our Manifestation for this day.

Shahnaz Kintz

Shahnaz Kintz grew up in a Bahá'í family of American background and was a Bahá'í pioneer in Africa. A graduate of Maxwell

International Bahá'í School, class of '02 she wrote this piece for an assignment at university.

Beyond Words

'A Bah-WHAT?' This phrase haunted my childhood. When questions of religion arose, I would inwardly cringe, knowing that, inevitably, I would be asked what Christian church I went to and knowing the look of confusion and fear that would soon appear on the faces of my peers when I would be forced to tell them that I was not a Christian at all but rather a Bahá'í. I would try to explain that it was a relatively new religion that believed in three main principles – that all mankind is created equal by God, that there is only one God and that all the religions come from the same God. Soon they would start to draw away and recoil in confusion... how could I NOT be a Christian? Didn't I know that only Christians were going to heaven? How could I not love Jesus Christ? I would try to explain that I did indeed believe in Jesus, just as I believed in Buddha, Moses and Muhammad. I also believed that God had sent us a new messenger, named Bahá'u'lláh, with new teachings for this day and age of humanity's development. Somehow, in my small town of Conway, South Carolina, where you were either Christian and saved or, well, you weren't, this explanation never really went over very well.

Despite my discomfort at being different and sticking out, I loved being a Bahá'í. I felt at home on Sunday mornings at the Bahá'í Centre, singing with my friends and their parents and saying prayers together. I looked forward to attending children's classes and couldn't wait to learn something new or memorize another prayer. I loved the principles of the Bahá'í Faith and I believed in them all. Things like men and women being created equal or the need for independent investigation of the truth just seemed to be common sense.

The summer after seventh grade marked a huge turning point in my life. My dad got a new job that moved our family to Liberia and I began a personal journey of my own. When originally asked, I had supported the decision, but when it came right down to it, I was terrified! I couldn't imagine leaving my town and my community and I was especially scared of going to Africa. Although I would be attending a boarding school in Canada with my sister, I would still be going to Liberia on all of my breaks and I wasn't sure how I felt about this idea. I was scared that we wouldn't have running water and that I would be forced to eat strange food and all of those other stereotypes we see on TV.

It wasn't until I met the Bahá'ís of Liberia that I learned all of my fears had been foolish. The first time I went to a Bahá'í meeting in Liberia, I was shocked. We were the only white people there but were instantly welcomed and made at home. Within seconds of entering the ramshackle building I felt as though I had known these people for years. Although the country was war-torn, with bullet holes decorating those buildings which hadn't been blown apart, when you got right down to it, the nation and its people weren't all that different from home. I started to realize that there was something amazing about this religion of mine that could bring people from such diverse backgrounds together in mere seconds and with such love between them all. It slowly dawned on me that maybe being a Bahá'í meant more than just playing with my friends and attending devotionals. Although I did begin to investigate the Bahá'í Faith for myself and really ask questions, I didn't truly start to understand the difference between being of the Bahá'í religion and *being* a Bahá'í until several years later, when I went to South Africa.

The Bahá'í Faith believes in the oneness of humanity – that we are all created by God to love and worship Him and that no person is created better or higher than anyone else. As such there is a lot of importance placed on service to others. Young people especially are encouraged to offer a period of service; whether it is a day at a community shelter or a year in another country, it is all valued. The focus is placed primarily on the youth because it is such a powerful time of transition for them. They are becoming independent from their family but are not yet tied down by responsibilities of their own. This is the time when you really start to develop your own personality and discover what you believe to be important and just.

After hearing this for my whole life and not having even a vague idea of what direction I wanted to take in college, I decided to take a year off and offer it as a time of service. I would focus on others and hopefully in the process discover something about myself. I explored several options and areas, from Thailand to Croatia, and eventually was drawn to a Bahá'í-run project in South Africa.

The project, called Beyond Words, was about finding solutions to social problems by going 'beyond words' and into action to solve them. Beyond Words was created as a performing arts group that travels around southern Africa, going into schools and communities with dances and skits about the various social issues affecting all of us today, and then taking it a step further. We talked to the students about how they could change their own lives. After a performance we would go into the classrooms and facilitate discussions to that end and then offer after-school meetings to go into the issues further. We were always very well received, especially after the kids realized that we were no different from any of them and we weren't there to tell them what they were doing wrong but to encourage what was right. At one school a student approached me with numerous questions about suicide. We talked for a long time about why anyone would want to commit suicide and how to help someone who is considering it. At the end of our talk, I found out that he himself had been very seriously considering the idea and through our conversation had made up his mind to seek help first.

The year I joined there were 12 of us from eight different countries: America, Canada, Ireland, Scotland, Germany, Albania, Taiwan and South Africa. We spent five intense weeks training and getting to know each other and then set off across the country in a dilapidated bus. Each place we went we were hosted by the Bahá'í community and were always welcomed like members of the family. Although every level of my being was tested during the year, I was happy. Even when we had very little food, were sleeping on cement floors and had no running water, I was content. For once I wasn't worrying about myself or what others thought of me. Instead, I was focused on empowering others to realize the difference they could make and the power they had over their own lives.

There is a saying, 'What does not kill you only makes you stronger.' I never truly believed that this could be true in both a physical and a spiritual sense until the past year. No matter what situation we found ourselves in, we always looked to God, remembered that we weren't there to please ourselves but rather Him, and we would pull through together. Even when our bus broke down one night in the middle of the desert, we managed to turn it into an adventure rather than a crisis. We spent the night stargazing, praying, singing and laughing until it finally became light enough to fix the bus temporarily.

The Bahá'í Faith is no longer an afterthought in my day. It has become my life and the centre of my focus. I am now concentrated on making my life fit around being a Bahá'í, rather than the opposite. Our world is sick and I want to help heal it – not by converting everyone to my view but by doing my part to help out my fellow brothers and sisters, whether they live in China, Afghanistan or right next door. I want to travel the world and help to empower those who have not been granted the same resources. Instead of cringing when I am asked about my religion and what I believe, I now become excited by the chance to share it with others. I look forward to the expression of surprise that flashes across people's faces. I love the challenge of soothing their fears that I am part of some devil-worshipping cult by explaining that, rather, I love all humanity as my own family and just want to make a difference in the world.

Fei-Lee Leong de Blanco

Fei-Lee Leong de Blanco currently resides in Australia, after having pioneered in Papua New Guinea and served in Latin America, where she met her husband.

I am Fei-Lee, the youngest daughter of Mariette and Ho-San Leong. I'm 24. I was blessed with having Bahá'í parents from two different cultural backgrounds. My mother is Australian and my dad is Chinese from Malaysia. I was born in Australia. However, from when I was about two until five years of age I lived in Papua New Guinea where my parents and family were pioneers. My family returned to the town I was born in, about an hour's drive out of Sydney, when I was six and it was at this time in my tender years that a consciousness of my identity started to emerge.

My dark hair, Asian eyes and Australian freckles made me different from everyone else at school. The small town where I lived with my parents and three siblings had limited diversity. There were no other Asian children at the primary school I went to except my own brother and myself. The only Chinese things people knew about were the small local Chinese restaurant on the main street and the radio advertisement for the 'Bing Lee' electrical appliance store.

I think that being different because of my Chinese heritage was a constant reminder of who I was, where I came from and why, which all boiled down to that fact that my parents were Bahá'ís and that I was a Bahá'í. Being a Bahá'í also meant that I went to a different scripture class at school every Tuesday morning and in the beginning it wasn't easy to be different. Actually it was sometimes difficult and painful. In the beginning I often got bullied by the boys and got into bitter fights and arguments. But with time I grew stronger and the name calling and prejudice stopped. Perhaps it was the stubbornness of my character or some intuitive God-given strength, but I never let the prejudice affect knowing that who I was, was a Bahá'í.

My closer friends knew that instead of going to church I sometimes went to a big white temple in Mona Vale (the Sydney Bahá'í House of Worship). I would tell my closer friends about going to feasts and about the unity of God and of religions and probably rambled on using big phrases like 'the equality of men and women' and 'progressive revelation', which they didn't understand but listened to before we continued to play another hand-clapping sing-a-long game or climb a tree.

Being the youngest child I grew up copying my siblings, especially my two older sisters, and I wanted to be just like them. I remember that my sisters danced and performed at Bahá'í concerts and conferences and participated in fun Bahá'í youth activities which I yearned to be a part of. I also loved to sing a few prayers that my mum taught me at an early age at feast and whenever we had Bahá'í friends over or met friends at Yerrinbool, a Bahá'í Institute. It was so exciting, interesting and fun.

When I was 11 my parents, brother and myself moved back to Papua New Guinea where I went to an international school with kids from all around the world. I think this reinforced my appreciation of diversity and love for Bahá'u'lláh's universal, world-embracing teachings. The Bahá'í community, youth classes and opportunities I had for meeting other wonderful Bahá'í pioneers all impacted on my Bahá'í identity and I feel this is what so motivated me years later to travel on my youth year of service. I went to the USA to participate in a Dance Workshop for six months and then to El Salvador in Central America for five months, where I taught children's classes and English classes, animated a Junior Youth Group and participated in countless nights of devotional meetings, study circles and more. It was there that I learned to speak Spanish and met my husband Ernesto, who was a Bahá'í youth in the Bahá'í community where I served. I am proud to be a second generation Bahá'í who, like my parents, has crossed the cultural boundary of marrying someone from across the other side of the world and who has hopefully helped to spread Bahá'u'lláh's teaching of unity in diversity for generations to come.

Each day of my life continues to confirm countless reasons why I am a Bahá'í. My parents brought me up as a Bahá'í and sowed the seed of love for Bahá'u'lláh within me from the beginning. The following recollection I have of a conversation I had with my mother when I was about nine years old is what comes to mind most when I think about how I automatically accepted and wanted to be a Bahá'í.

My mother was talking to me about what services I could do for Bahá'u'lláh when I grew up and, as a child does, I said to her with my tongue in cheek and a grin on my face, 'What if I don't believe in Bahá'u'lláh?'

She paused and looked at me dubiously but confidently and said, 'I would be surprised if you didn't.'

The fact was, I knew it was a silly question – and she did too.

A WARM PLACE IN MY HEART

Aletha Phillips

Aletha currently attends Canterbury High School in Ottawa, Ontario. She specializes in the vocal programme at Canterbury, which is a school dedicated to learning through the arts, and while it is a public school, admission is by audition only.

'What is it to be a Bahá'í?' I ask my Sunday school class. They are a great group of six and seven year olds. When asked this question most of them give puzzled looks, twiddle their fingers or are just distracted by something else and say nothing. I look around at the other two teachers who teach the class and they look just as puzzled. 'Is the point of being a Bahá'í to lie all the time and get what we want?' I ask jokingly. All the kids laugh but still say nothing. I realize that this is the one subject that we've covered that none of the kids have anything to say about. Even the troublemaker in the class, who would usually have something funny to say, is silent. They all look at me as though I should have the answer – they are just little children and I will make sense of why they are Bahá'ís. But I can't. The whole class just sits there for a few minutes, as each teacher tries to come up with something good to say, but none of us can find the words. I end up using some explanation like, 'We are Bahá'ís because we believe in Bahá'u'lláh.' Although this commonly-used phrase is true, it doesn't really explain why one would devote his life to serving God.

As I went home I continued to think about why I would want to be a Bahá'í. It's hard being one in North America. Outside the Bahá'í community I don't think that I have one friend who doesn't either drink on a regular basis or do drugs often. Maybe its just that I'm friends with the wrong people but that's how it is for me. I think about how I have to turn everything down and be the only person out of my friends who isn't 'trashed' on Friday night. The thought of this is not really a problem but more the action of it, not to mention not backbiting, praying every day, being chaste and being honest all the time. These things are all hard to deal with but they still don't deter me from saying that I am a Bahá'í. So I kept wondering, what is so great about it that I'd want to live my life differently from everyone else.

Then it kind of dawned on me. I'm a Bahá'í because it's who I am. Not being a Bahá'í would just be a lie for me. Having grown up in a Bahá'í family, my values and opinions are all based on the Bahá'í Faith. All my life I've gone to firesides that my mother hosts at the info centre every Friday, I attend every feast and go to children's classes every Sunday morning. When as a pre-teen I tried to turn away from it and ignore its values and laws, I ended up not being able to. I came back to the Faith because it's who I am. Most people come to the Faith on their own, which has its benefits as well, but being born into a Bahá'í family is one of the best gifts you can get because you are born with it. It becomes a part of you. The Faith may not always exactly reflect how I see the world but, hey, I don't know everything. When I'm faced with troubles and difficulties, I'm not afraid because I know that it's part of me, guiding me along the way. So why am I a Bahá'í? Because it's a part of me that I want other people to have as a part of them. So in wanting to do so, I must spread the message of Bahá'u'lláh.

Celeste Gómez

Celeste Gómez is the eldest of five children born to a Honduran father and Canadian mother who met and married while serving at the Bahá'í World Centre in the early 1990s. Subsequently they returned to Central America, where Celeste was born. The family pioneered to Honduras and Belize until 2004, when they home front pioneered to a small, wintry city in northern British Columbia,. It is from there that Celeste offered her thoughts as she turned 15.

Why I am a Bahá'í

My name is Celeste Gómez. I am 15 years old and live in northern British Columbia. I have lived in Honduras and Belize and now live in Canada. I speak both English and Spanish and I'm learning French.

I have been a Bahá'í all my life and I am really privileged to be able to say that. I think that being a Bahá'í has been one of the few things that has made me who I am today. It's really important to me. There are times when I wish I was normal and fitted in with everyone else but deep down I'm glad that I'm not. I find that being a Bahá'í teen in Canada is not easy, especially when you live in an undeveloped city and you're not as informed as you should be. One of the reasons why I am a Bahá'í is because I love people and I love the world and I think that being a Bahá'í brings me closer to helping people and the world.

I have seen a lot of things that I wish I had never seen but at the same time I'm glad that I have because that's what makes me able to connect with people and teach them about others and why they should care.

I was born into an interracial marriage. My dad is from Honduras and my mom is from Canada. I think that that has helped me be able to accept other races more and have a better cultural understanding. I am a Bahá'í because I have been raised as one and lived as one my entire life and to say that I am not a Bahá'í would be a lie that I don't believe. I'm really lucky to be who I am.

Compiler's note: Following this report, I asked Celeste to respond to some specific questions. Here are her answers:

1. *What do you remember most about being a Bahá'í in Honduras?*

I remember taking a drive down to the city in my dresses and going to feasts and events. There weren't many other children but I liked to read prayers and sing lots of songs.

I remember when Hurricane Mitch hit and my parents went out to help the people whose houses had been destroyed.

I loved to go to Bahá'í houses and watch my parents talk about important things.

I remember helping people, my friends, and loving to say my prayers.

2. *What do you think about the Bahá'í community in Belize?*

I think that the Bahá'í community in San Ignacio and Santa Elena was great. Everyone was enthusiastic and ready to do things. Everyone was really involved and I think that it was growing very well thanks to the youth from the US and Canada. I think they really helped and got local people involved. The Faith was growing at a rapid pace and I loved the energy that I felt whenever I went to gatherings.

3. *What things do you think are the similarities between young people your own age in the three countries you have lived in?*

I think that people my age in these countries are really similar. In all these countries I find that we were all very mature but in different ways. In Honduras we were taught to be respectful and reverent. In Belize we were very involved with people and our level of knowledge increased. In Canada I think that kids know more about the world and aren't as sheltered as teens in Honduras and Belize.

4. *How do you think that being a Bahá'í helps the world?*

Being a Bahá'í helps the world in a way I can't describe. The best I can say is that we use our judgement wisely and have a different way of seeing things. That helps because if the way others see things doesn't work then we can help them see things in a different way.

~~~~~~~

Thomas Mitchell Doran and Tim Doran

Thomas Mitchell Doran is the youngest of a family of five children. Tim is his older brother. Mitchell expressed himself in prose, while Tim is a talented singer-songwriter and shared a song lyric in answer to my request for a contribution. Both currently reside at home in Saskatoon, Saskatchewan. Thomas wrote me with this descrip-

tion of himself: 'This was written by Thomas Doran, a boy born in Saskatchewan, the youngest of five children, and a voice from the outside of the crowd.'

I'd have to say that the thing I treasure most about being a Bahá'í is the fact that the youth of today know how to have fun without drinking or smoking and I know in today's society it's a tough thing to do. I find that one of the key reasons I consider myself a Bahá'í is the youth, because when you have friends you're confident they're going to call you when there's a party, and when they are going to a youth conference, they will invite you to ride with them even though you're two or more years younger than them. It makes you think, imagine if everyone in the world were like them – guaranteed it still wouldn't be perfect but it'd be a lot better.

On days of feasts I walk into the room where it's being held and I don't feel nervous. I'm greeted with smiles not glares. So to me unity is definitely what made me a Bahá'í. Being a former victim of bullying, it's heaven knowing everyone is a lifelong friend.
Thomas Mitchell Doran

There is no protest here
We are born and die against will.
Place the flag at a half-mast
Declare Him the winning side
It is not a choice of Faith but arrogance.
What is destined is that
and in the final end
Fate is disposable as the skin we're in
So kill the optimist

Shove elixir down his oesophagus
You ask me why I've chosen this way
I can only inquire
Is there another path or thicket to mull through?
Tim Doran

A WARM PLACE IN MY HEART

Robert Gillies

My name is Robert Gillies. I am 21 and originally from Scotland. I am currently pursuing a musical dream and serving at the Maxwell International School in B.C., Canada.

So, why, in this day and age, do I choose to be a Bahá'í?

I was introduced to the Bahá'í Faith at the age of seven and all I remember is readily accepting the Faith because I felt welcomed and at ease. Now you might think that accepting something like the Faith at the age of seven because you feel accepted is a little strange but I had a hard time at school and so in some subconscious and spiritual sense I must have resonated with the Revelation of Bahá'u'lláh.

I'm now 21 years old and it's been 14 years since my mother declared and showed me the Faith and I do ask myself 'why?' every so often. I think that with each passing day my reasons increase in number as my understanding of the Faith increases. Being a Bahá'í allows you to view the world from an incredibly objective viewpoint and so allows you to approach life with an open mind, an open heart and a certainty that the world is on its way to something greater. Whereas many people read the news and despair at the state of the world's disrepair, Bahá'ís not only know that it's going to get worse but that it needs to get worse to get better.

I honestly don't know where I'd be without the Faith. I know I'd be religious because my parents raised me in such a way and for that I am ever thankful. But would I, in my teenage years, have strayed? Most probably. Being a Bahá'í I had countless writings to refer to, to read and meditate on for help and guidance. Not only this but Bahá'u'lláh laid down so many wonderful laws and ordinances that are there for our protection and prosperity. So many people view laws as restraints but how many of those people can say that they truly follow laws? For instance, concerning alcohol and drugs, the Kitáb-i-Aqdas explicitly condemns the use of these substances. I look at so many of my old friends and acquaintances who drink and dabble in drugs and it saddens me greatly. I once went to a party where everyone but myself and one other friend (who happened to be a Bahá'í) was either drunk or on the way to being drunk. One girl ended up weeping for no apparent reason, another threw up in the sink repeatedly, while others wrestled or fell asleep where they ended up. If that isn't depressing to anyone, what is? It's obvious why we need to steer clear of such substances. You lose proper perspective on life and yourself, a self which it is your responsibility to look after.

At this point one can introduce another beautiful aspect of the Revelation, a point regarding the nobility of the human spirit. If people could even start to fathom our spiritual stations and journeys I reckon drugs and the like would go straight out the window.

For me there is no shorthand answer for why I am a Bahá'í in this day and age but I will say this: The Faith provides hope, solace and courage. It provides humanity with the power to reach heights that even the greatest spiritual minds cannot grasp. In an instant, night can become day, sadness become joy, a stranger become a friend and the world become one country. Differences are beautiful, all races are one and the love of God prevails in even the darkest of nights! Yá Bahá'u'l-Abhá!

Matt Fillmore

Matt Fillmore is a graduate of the University of Western Ontario (class of 2006), where he studied Music Education and English. He is passionate about justice, peace and the human soul, and became a Bahá'í at the age of 18. Currently, he is working as a teacher at the Bahá'í-inspired School of the Nations in Macau.

I am 23 years old and became a Bahá'í when I was 18. I lived in Ottawa, Ontario. At the time of becoming a Bahá'í I didn't know much more than that the Faith brought calm to my heart in a way that nothing else did. It seemed right, so I did it. My declaration occurred five days before I left for university, so many things changed at that time: my school, my friends, my home and my Faith were all 'renovated', so to speak.

While at university, in London, Ontario, I became involved with the Bahá'í community and participated in the Ruhi curriculum, devotional meetings and children's classes. These were my primary activities throughout university – the 'main course' of my life then.

For the last two years I have had a restless feeling in my heart and that has shown itself in a deep-seated desire to travel. In the summer of 2004 I went to Pennsylvania to work at a summer camp. I had a good time, generally, but I found it very spiritually draining, as it was a secular camp with very few opportunities for prayer or personal time. In the summer of 2005 I went to Yellowknife to do service with the Bahá'í community up there. That time was a transformative period in my life: it was the first time I had moved to a place with the sole purpose of serving the community and I found that having that mind set and maintaining it helped me to understand what service really meant – total focus on teaching the Cause, uplifting human hearts and serving the Faith and its interests.

Most recently, in August 2006, I pioneered to Macau, China, and am currently working as a teacher at the School of the Nations, a Bahá'í-inspired school here. I am finding the school to be a very inspiring place to work – the differences between Bahá'í-inspired educational practice and the broader society's educational practice are very challenging and illuminating – and I am finding that Macau's population are very warm with receptive hearts.

Compiler's note: I followed up this initial piece from Matt with some questions, to which he replied in detail in December 2006.

1. How did you first hear of the Bahá'í Faith and do you think you were pre-inclined to be interested or was it something specific that attracted you?

I first heard of the Bahá'í Faith from a friend of mine named Amber Phelan. She is about the same age as me and at the time (summer 2000), we were both in high school. Initially, I dismissed the Bahá'í Faith as 'just another religion'. I saw religions as a source of, rather than a solution to, conflict. I couldn't understand how faiths that spent so much time speaking about peace could fight so often and

I decided the best thing to do was to ignore them entirely. That changed, however, when I took a philosophy course in my last semester of high school (January to June 2001). We spent a good deal of time talking about important moral and political questions and since faith and philosophy are so closely connected, we often noticed similarities between our ideas of 'right and wrong' and the ideas put forward by major religions. At that point I became very curious about the Faith and started asking many questions. The philosophy course acted like a catalyst, using my deep-seated concerns about moral and political issues to point me towards religion. Was I pre-inclined to be interested in it? Yes – once I saw the connections between the concerns of society and the concerns of religion, I had a restless desire to learn more.

2. *What did you study at university and can you share any anecdotes from that time which were especially confirming in your decision to commit to the Faith?*

At university, I completed an honours degree in Music Education and focused my non-music studies on English Literature and Language. The greatest experiences I had in university were all connected with the Bahá'í community. Though I was involved with service at my campus residences and in the university community, it was always the service done with the Bahá'ís that felt most selfless and most satisfying. There is no specific event that comes to mind; rather, I think fondly of musical programmes prepared for feasts, lessons prepared for children's classes, food and drink shared with the community, spiritual discussions with friends who were curious about the Bahá'ís and the many other experiences.

3. *Can you talk more about the link between your travels and your spiritual development? What do Bahá'í activities offer you that others do not?*

Primarily, my travels have been very important to the growth of my spirit because they have, in a very physical, concrete way, changed my perspective on spiritual matters. For example, my summer 2005 period of service in Yellowknife, Northwest Territories, meant that I travelled 3000 kilometres from my home to a place that was totally unfamiliar to me for the sole purpose of serving the Bahá'í Faith. As a result, I had no homework, no socializing to do, no apartment to worry about – all the concerns that would typically have occupied my thoughts at home were not present. For the first time in my life, my days began with the question, 'How can I serve Bahá'u'lláh today?' I stopped thinking of service as an activity for which I had to set aside time and began thinking of it as the underlying motive for any activity I undertook.

This realization illustrates what Bahá'í activities have given me: gradually, the line separating my 'Bahá'í life' from my 'life' has dissolved to the point where I now feel that my primary reason for being is to live as a Bahá'í. This means undertaking activities with the love of Bahá'u'lláh in my heart, keeping my sights set on teaching His Faith and striving to follow His guidance. Of course, I have times when I feel that I'm not living up to these standards but I view such times as learning experiences, for two reasons: they illumine my frailties, to show me how I can improve, and they underscore how much I really do want to live up to Bahá'u'lláh's standards.

4. *Have you found any challenges to your faith in the years since your declaration? If so, how have you handled them?*

The biggest challenges to my faith have all come from within myself. I have never had a 'crisis of faith', in the stereotypical sense ('why is God doing this to me?'). Rather, the challenges to my faith existed as a kind of background tension over a long period of time. For example, I found it challenging, in university, to choose between becoming involved in campus life (working for the university residence system, volunteering with the university orientation programme) and becoming involved in the Bahá'í community. I was involved in both to varying degrees throughout my time as a student and both brought me satisfaction, but, as I said earlier, I invariably found involvement with the Bahá'í community more fulfilling. However, my three-year employment with the university residence system (which paid for my accommodation) took significant chunks of my time and there were times when I longed to give more to the Bahá'í community. Such times were challenging because I felt as though I was not a part of the ongoing efforts to teach the Faith and, overall, I felt as though I was not living up to my obligations as a Bahá'í. I was ashamed. On reflection, I think I could have done more to fix that: I could have made a better effort to manage my time and my work effectively. Nevertheless, I was usually able to pull myself out of such slumps by becoming involved in some form of service to the Bahá'í community, which always lifted and refocused my spirit.

Olinga Martel

Olinga is the son of a French-Canadian father and an East Indian mother. Olinga was born in Africa and the family have spent their lives as Bahá'í pioneers to various African countries. Olinga speaks Portuguese owing to his years in Cape Verde and French because of his father and his years in French-speaking Africa. A graduate of Maxwell International Bahá'í School's class of '99, he shared glimpses of his life in Africa through personal correspondence, which he has given me permission to excerpt and reproduce here.

23 December 2001

I know you like to have updates on what each of us is doing as the time passes. Well, I am now an unemployed commercial pilot and I have been looking for work for some time although not very successfully. I have been doing other things while looking for work. I participated in a two-week Ruhi book 6 training course in South Africa and I have been facilitating a bit for a couple of the Ruhi books here in Lesotho. The Lesotho Bahá'í summer school just ended. I was responsible for the children's programme and enjoyed the great difficulty of having a mixed group from five years of age to 16, which was fun. I am now off to the international summer school in Swaziland where I will do nothing but participate and enjoy it.

I have made a very important decision in my life, a spiritual commitment: to pioneer. I contacted the pioneer committee for Africa and offered my services to pioneer and they replied yesterday giving guidance. Since I speak Portuguese I will be looking to pioneer in either Mozambique or the very small São Tomé and Principe. My approach will be to travel teach, starting in Mozambique . . . and at the same time look at opportunities for work. If I find work, I will establish myself permanently there. If not, I will travel teach in São Tomé and Principe after my pilgrimage in the second half of April and see what the opportunities are like there for sustenance. I pray that Bahá'u'lláh will guide me and that I will fulfil what He wants for me. This is a very personal thing and I am by no means asking for praise and hopefully don't come across as being boastful, just sharing. This is a lifetime commitment for me for the continent of Africa, for now they need me in either one of the two Portuguese speaking countries . . .

South Africa is really in a very sick state, deeply lost in materialism. Many are truly sick: we hear stories of groups of adults raping children as young as four months old and the shootings are forever going on. I, myself, living in a house out in the bush away from town in Port Elizabeth, had a bullet through the window.

9 January 2002

It's funny how things happened in Swazi for me. It's funny in the sense that I had plans to stay at a Backpackers in Mbabane near the location of the summer school and I ran into a friend and ended up staying at his house in Mbabane. I had never imagined all that . . .

My family is well. My sister will finish I.B.2 in June (International Bacheloria, it's like 'A' levels in the UK. It's her grade 12, if comparing to Canada), then she plans to do a year of service at the Bahá'í school in the Czech Republic, then go to Canada to study and become a 'forensic detective' after years of hard work.

My parents are planning to stay in Lesotho for at least another two years, in the mountains where there is a great need for pioneers, and if my mother is okay with the coldish winters then I think they will stay there. Now we are in the city because of Rani's schooling. Me, you know me. Desperately looking for work in São Tomé or Mozambique where I will pioneer. The Martel gang, we are, all in all, doing well.

You asked if I have friends here to socialize with. No, I don't. I spend my time either at home studying advanced aviation subjects/Bahá'í literature or teaching/facilitating Ruhi 1, 2 or 6 and doing children's classes. And I went to that summer school. But I am off to Mozambique beginning in February and that will be a new chapter, continuing from where I stopped when I lived in the north of Mozambique for three years. There is another voice saying, 'Be open to São Tomé e Principe as well', and the greatest needs are most likely there but I have some chance of finding work in Mozambique and have no idea about São Tomé. We will know in April how things end up in Mozambique. I pray for guidance.

I do strongly believe – and maybe I am one of those very naive Bahá'ís – that through my service to the Faith God will guide me and help me out with my needs in life (or bounties), and hopefully He will see the need for me to get married and I will be able to have that in my life. My current up-to-date conclusion on all that is, I continue to serve the Faith, make friends and I hope to marry by 25 and finish having three kids by 30. Obviously I am not the only decision-maker in that and it depends on me being able to provide but those are my goals/dreams. Don't get me wrong, the mother can provide too but I do feel it to be one of my duties. Bahá'u'lláh will guide me, God willing. The rest is a mystery, although I do fancy talking about it all and get carried away all the time.

I suppose I have made pioneering my first dream; the next, my marriage. My heart already belongs to Bahá'u'lláh; the rest I can give to my family.

Some people come and go; others touch our hearts and we are never ever the same.

Keep well and please send my regards to your family and friends when you see them. If you ever want to find me, look in Africa, I will always be here, 'God willing'. I feel it's where I am needed.

22 January 2002

I have been busy with teaching Ruhi 2 and now I am preparing a study of the House of Justice message of April 1998 on Training Institutes. Right after that I will be helping the same group become tutors for books 1 and 2. Just a bit busy but I enjoy it. Anyway, it's a bit of a rush since I am leaving for Mozambique in two weeks.

I hope life is treating you well and that the family is also doing well. I suppose everyone has grown and continues to grow. It just actually hit me a couple of days ago that I am never going to be younger. In March I will be 21 and the pressure is on to live the adult life. I will never forget the winter that I spent with my grandfather in Quebec in St Ramould. He has a house right on the St Lawrence River, just down the river from the 'Quebec bridge', and it is such a beautiful place. It is the sort of place where you just reflect so much and dream. We were talking one sunny winter afternoon and he was telling me stories of his youth. At some point he told me, 'It's all gone by so fast' and it's true. For me just eight years ago I was learning to speak and write English, and suddenly three years ago I graduated. Then came university, then becoming a commercial pilot, then I made my dream come true with my decision to pioneer. What's next? Marriage? Kids? Only God knows. But in the end it's all spiritual growth for my soul that will continue its journey into the next world. What an adventure and how much growth and development goes on from childhood to old age!

I do feel that I am prepared to face the tests to come although it's part of the growing process and it will be a life-lasting thing. I don't feel like anyone can be fully prepared, although I do trust in God. I resort to prayer as a source of inspiration and assistance with tests . . . I always feel inadequate for pioneering. I can wait five years to study the Faith more then pioneer but if I go now and start with what I have and experience the tests and growth I will face, I do feel that five years from now my level of growth and experience will be much more than if I waited until I was more knowledgeable. Teaching is learning and learning is teaching. When you teach, 90% of teaching goes to the teacher and 10%

to the hearer. I mean, it's in itself the process. I don't know if I lost you but I think all in all you understand me.

4 February 2002

I am writing a short note from Mozambique. I arrived a few days ago, safe and sound. The trips are not so easy but we eventually get to our destinations, with a lot of exercise sometimes, but it is all part of the adventure. I can't wait to have my own little aeroplane to fly around. Maybe in 20 years' time.

29 April 2002

I was in Mozambique for two months travel teaching and trying to find work so that I can fulfil the need for a pioneer there and answer the call of the Universal House of Justice for pioneers in various parts of the world. Like Hand of the Cause Dr Varqa told us during our pilgrimage, 'The Universal House of Justice needs our help to fulfil the goals of the Faith.' I suppose that would be for all the needs within our capacities.

I just returned from a very wonderful pilgrimage with my family and 106 other wonderful pilgrims. Guess who was in my pilgrim group? Luke Baumgartner![3] It was very nice to see him! Wonderful.

Being there was like being under this huge safe shelter in the middle of crossfire, 'war'. I was standing in Bahjí one day listening to the familiar sounds of aircraft flying about in the sky but then I realized they weren't so familiar. I noticed that what I was hearing belonged to a specific group of aircraft, which served only one purpose, that of fighting. As I looked up I could see them sending missiles, two at a time, to the north and then turning back. I wondered what was lying north and after a few questions to the locals I realized it was Lebanon. What a shame, I thought. But as 'guests of Bahá'u'lláh' I was sure that I had nothing to worry about. If the Universal House of Justice didn't tell us to cancel the pilgrimage it must have been perfectly all right.

We were fortunate to be 'in the spiritual presence' of the Báb,

---

3 Compiler's note: A mutual friend from Maxwell, who has also contributed to this book.

Bahá'u'lláh, 'Abdu'l-Bahá, some of the faithful holy family, the Universal House of Justice as an institution, the two living Hands of the Cause of God, the members of the International Teaching Centre and of course, for the first day of Riḍván celebration, the staff of the World Centre. To be honest I also felt the presence of my older sister Uma, whom I long to hug in the next world. I had that experience in the Shrine of Bahá'u'lláh and it was not only me – everyone in our little family mentioned it. Some felt it in the Shrine of the Báb and some in recalling 'Abdu'l-Bahá.

I think you have heard time and time again and perhaps you have experienced it yourself that pilgrimage is truly unique. Hand of the Cause Furútan said, although I have never read it, that we will only fully understand the significance of pilgrimage in the next world.

15 May 2002

If I weren't a Bahá'í I would spend a lot of time mountain biking around the world and mountaineering in our beautiful mountains – the Antarctic mountains and others like Everest, Kilimanjaro. For now I will continue to climb in my dreams and wake up on the floor wondering which mountain I fell off! Maybe we could actually get a few Bahá'ís living on the top of those places! Then I could climb the mountains and still visit Bahá'ís and give Ruhi classes.

Perhaps a bit farfetched!

29 May 2002

I have offered up my life to Bahá'u'lláh in His service as a pioneer in Africa. I feel really strongly about that but maybe Bahá'u'lláh wants me somewhere else and if that were the case I would be ready tomorrow to pack and go wherever He says 'GO'. I know I could serve anywhere and that would be perfectly fine with me but I have a feeling that I would be most useful in Africa, given my present experience. I humbly requested Him to show me the way. I hope I have the eyes to see.

I have already offered up my life for the Faith and I need a partner who will join me in this journey. Of course, I hope to be blessed with a family and that will have its own implications when it comes to decision-making as to where and when and how. I hope that she has similar needs and we can complement each other. I trust that God will provide. I pray that I will see these signs that you mentioned and that my service to the Faith will be acceptable to God.

15 November 2002

I am happy to hear that everything is normal on your side of the world, although the cold is setting in. We, of course, on this side of the hemisphere are enjoying a nice summer. I must apologize again for not having written in such a long while. Can't say that I have any good excuses to give you.

I am doing all right, can't complain although still facing the tests of life. Who isn't? I am still without work at the moment although I was offered a job in Mozambique and maybe next year around March I will start it if the job is still around then. We shall see.

I continue to travel back and forth from Lesotho through South Africa to Mozambique. The last couple of months I was in Mozambique and now I am back in Lesotho spending some time at home. I ran into a friend from Maxwell I hadn't seen for six odd years and hadn't been in touch with . . . who is also trying to pioneer in Mozambique but also finding it difficult to find work. He is in human rights. He is also finding Portuguese hard to learn . . .

I was reading some things about the marriage of 'Abdu'l-Bahá and it has left quite a huge impression in my mind. He says, 'But the love which sometimes exists between friends is not (true) love, because it is subject to transmutation; this is merely fascination.' It goes on, 'Today you will see two souls apparently in close friendship; tomorrow all this may be changed. Yesterday they were ready to die for another, today they shun one another's society!' ('Abdu'l-Bahá, *Paris Talks*, p. 181) Interesting stuff. Just that word in there 'fascination' started an interesting thought process in my mind . . .

26 July 2003

Marriage. To be honest with you I have been spending much of my thoughts on that and am keeping an eye out but haven't yet found anyone who wants to share the kind of life I would like to live. I can't marry someone whose dreams and goals in life are to go and live in Europe or Canada. Nothing wrong with that but my heart is set for Africa and I will bury my bones in Africa. Hopefully sooner rather than later (marry, that is) but I suppose it will come. I'm 22 and time is passing by so fast. Surely one day I will have the pleasure to give you the news. Until then, what a mystery.

26 August 2003

I am travelling on Wednesday, most likely to Swaziland by 'Combi' (mini-van type thing) and will stay three days then come back and prepare for my trip to Zambia. Yes, I am off to Zambia on the job hunt again. If I get something there in aviation I'll take it and, being a neighbour to Angola and Mozambique, I can give support to both, then after a year try to go back to Angola more permanently. If not, then it looks like I will end up being 'country manager' for SMEC International (Engineering Consultancy) in Angola doing things that have nothing to do with aviation for a year initially but at least I'll be able to stay in Angola and while I am there I'll keep on trying. It's conditional on me going back there. A Bahá'í I know very well is the manager for Africa and doesn't have an office in Angola unless I do it. That's why it's so flexible and dependent on me.

That's it. We shall see what I end up doing. We are cooking ideas again and we shall see what we end up making. Hopefully it will have a nice taste . . .

As you said about marriage, my time too will come and I shall tell you the wonderful news . . . It's really difficult to find 'someone who is ready' for this kind of life (by no means is this better or superior to any other way of life) and, when you do, it does not mean that you can necessarily live the rest of your life with that person. I just always remember what 'Abdu'l-Bahá says, that we must with 'utmost care' investigate each other's characters. Well you can just imagine the state of our society (Africa) by looking at the AIDS statistics, for example. Of course, they choose to generalize and there are millions of wonderful people but our society is sick. Lesotho where I live has 35% of its two million population HIV+. This is a reflection, I feel, of the low level of moral education and also means not enough people know about Bahá'u'lláh and His remedy.

God willing I will recognize God's greater plan for me and that soon I may follow it and choose it. I don't know if we can ever be ready enough. I for one know nothing about pioneering and it is really like just jumping in the ocean, then learning to swim. I know the tide will get rough sometimes but I know that for my survival I need to breathe and my spiritual oxygen has to be obedience, steadfastness and reliance on God.

Lots of people are playing games and pretending to be adults. I don't play games with feelings and always make things very clear because once you feed those feelings and imaginations, if it doesn't work out you end up unhappy. It's the time to study now as it is when children are very young that it is time to play and to sing 'O God, My God', as 'Abdu'l-Bahá says.

19 October 2003

I have met my beloved and we have been seeing each other seriously, going out for about a month, although we have been good friends for some time. I guess I have a girlfriend for the first time in my life. It doesn't stop there. I am planning on getting married in April next year. We have decided and we are busy working on the consent, although it all seems to be good to go.

I must say I was never satisfied with the counsel that you gave that you 'just know' but now I understand and see it as the best explanation, as it is exactly the case; you can't explain love. We are both committed and have similar desires in life in terms of service to the Faith and our love for Africa. Her name is Nontsiki (short for Nontsikelelo). We are very committed to each other and have really a wonderful and clear channel of communication going on between the two of us, as we have been studying the compilation on marriage. We realized how we are great combination, the two of us.

She is the environmental coordinator for Sechaba Consultants. I guess one thing that is coming as a great surprise is that my wedding will not be a small wedding as I had wished but will be big because her family is really huge. In only the immediate family we counted about 87 and there must be double that that we have to invite! My side will be just my parents and, I hope, my sister, if she can leave UVIC and come. We shall see.

2 June 2004

The wedding went very well. We did our civil marriage around 9:00 on that Saturday and then the Bahá'í wedding started at 11:00 and at 12:30 we had the luncheon and everything was finished by 16:00. It was very big; it was bigger than I had ever wanted or dreamed of but that is how they are here and our families are very big and extend beyond the nuclear family. On my side it was just my parents and a few friends but on Nontsiki's side there were many. We had around 500 people at our wedding. I guess it was a good proclamation since maybe 30 were Bahá'ís. No alcohol and people still had a wonderful time. Lots of fun. The following weekend my parents killed two sheep and gave a reception way up in the mountains where they live. They invited the friends around there and there were about 100 people. I say way up because it is very far up. It takes about five hours from the capital, Maseru, although it's only about 300 km.

Family life is wonderful and we are learning a lot about each other and of course about married life. With time our family of two will hopefully increase but of course all in good time. I look forward to having the little ones around one day.

21 September 2004

It has been a while since we have been in touch. I won't apologize because it's starting to sound like a broken record but I will thank you for writing.

My wife and I are very well, happy and healthy. We are excited and time is passing so fast, March is coming closer and closer by the day and soon our family will have grown. Everyone seems to have premonitions that our first child will be a boy and just for the heck of it I am betting on a girl. If it's a boy his name will be Leseli, pronounced Le-se-di (means light) and if we have a girl she will most likely be Sipho Sihle, meaning beautiful gift.

We don't dream and really do not plan on twins but should it be the case we will embrace it.

23 September 2004

My parents are doing very well and, yes, they will be grandparents next year in March, God willing. Nontsiki's health is good and she is being followed up carefully every month. We are confident that things will be okay. Most definitely the news can be shared.

Nontsiki and I would like to visit next year in your summer, around June, July, but of course all this depends on our finances. I would love to travel together with my parents. I dream of flying to Quebec then driving across to Vancouver to see Rani then fly out from there. Anyway, all in good time.

What have I been doing? Well, I have been busy the last three weeks building. It involved renovating an old house made of corrugated iron. I closed a door and opened more windows, pulled down walls to make larger rooms and put in other walls to create space for things like a bathroom. I fixed the leaks on the roof then worked on the ceiling and walls inside with wood, flooring boards actually. Looks good. I hope the boss will be happy. I have finished that and cannot wait to receive my earnings for that work. I have also started a small business. I make paper of different kinds and colours and make albums, diaries, cards, wedding invitation cards and that sort of thing, using a bit of my artistic skills. Of course I am still a pilot and I am continuously trying to get work. There are some leads I am following up and hopefully one of them will materialize. We would like to buy a house instead of paying rent, so the material means are in great need at the moment but we cannot complain, we are really doing well and living comfortably.

This coming weekend we are having a conference called 'Extreme Momentum'. I guess it's a play on words from 'Building Momentum'. It is organized by the National Teaching Committee of South Africa. Should be fun meeting friends from around. You never know, we might meet some visitors from faraway Canada that we may know.

Life is going on well for us. We have our obstacles to overcome but God is helping us. I will keep you in my prayers and I hope you will really be successful with your writing. I remember Kiser Barnes telling Rani, 'You know the Faith really needs a lot of good writers.' He was encouraging her to pursue writing as opposed to being a forensic detective which she is doing.

10 March 2005

I have been extremely busy these last couple of weeks as you may soon understand. My wife is due any time soon so we hope that we shall have been increased by one very, very soon. We are very excited and I will send you a photo of the baby as soon as I have it available. I have told my wife and the baby and hope that we have a good understanding that I don't wish to share my birthday with a member of my family, so we shall see how things turn out. I am born on the 17th and it is coming very close.

I am very keen to see what kind of genes this child will choose from my wife and me and what he or she will look like.

5 April 2005

Hi Granny Heather!
How are you doing? Hope all is well with you.

Leseli Louis Lusanda Martel was born on the 15th of March 2005. He was 3.385 kg and 50 cm tall at birth and is eating very well. We are all very happy at home and happy to have an addition to our family.

Let me explain to you the name: Leseli (means 'light', Sesotho), Louis (my grandfather's name, French), Lusanda (means 'the family has been increased', Xhosa) and Martel, well, that I don't have to explain.

I am very happy to finally be a father and am really enjoying every moment of it. Some days and nights are more difficult than others but all in all it's nothing terrible. The most difficult thing is when he cries and you don't know how to help him; that must be the worst feeling in the world but, hey, it's part of it.

Sorry this note is very short. I am just writing to let you know of this great happening. All my prayers have been answered, including the one requesting that he not be born on my birthday (17th). I wanted him to have his own birthday.

A WARM PLACE IN MY HEART

26 September 2006

Hi Heather,
Hope all is well with you. I am sorry I haven't been able to write to you and even now I will only be able to write a short note . . . Nontsiki is out in the field and will not be available for the next two weeks. She is busy relocating a village where a diamond mine is going to be digging for precious stones. She cannot be reached before she comes back.

9 October 2006

I am still waiting for Nontsiki to come back. By the way, she doesn't work with diamonds, she works with people. The people have to be relocated because of the mine and she is doing the social and environmental impact assessment. Just wanted to clear that up.

10 October 2006

I am indeed interested in film making and animation; storytelling in those media are my second major interests after aviation, which right now has not worked out. I shot a short film in August which I am still busy editing, about a migrant labourer from Lesotho working in the mines of South Africa. It is HIV/AIDS related. I make extra money by doing graphic design and videos for events like weddings and the like. I work every day, though, in a photo lab as a technician and custom framer. Just letting you know what I do these days since I have been out of touch for so long.

17 February 2007

My wife and I received a blessing from God a few days ago, a little girl. Siphosihle Carmel Martel was born on the 15th of February 2007 at 18:27 weighing 2.8 kgs. She is such a beautiful gift as is the meaning of her name (Siphosihle is beautiful gift in Xhosa) and although we know that she may look like an old lady in her early days, we are very proud parents. She is very sweet and hardly cries. She can lay awake without crying and although we know that big brother will show her how 'naughty' is done when she is older, for now we are very happy to get a little rest.

We were worried about our son Leseli, who is going to be two years old on the 15th of March, how he was going to react, but he has been quite understanding it seems and very excited. It took him a few days to figure out than he couldn't hold her too strongly but he is now getting it right. Plenty of kisses and a lot of laughter.

Just wanted to give you the good news and send our greetings to you and your family.

Much love,
Olinga Martel

Amelia Dana

Amelia Dana was born in Papua New Guinea to American pioneer parents and is currently living in the Netherlands with her husband Shahram. Her life adventure continues and her entry speaks for itself.

While many people may often feel the intense love, beauty and spirit of the Bahá'í Faith when they go on a nine day pilgrimage to the Holy Land, I feel blessed to have been exposed to a similar and uniquely amazing spirit from a culture and country in which I grew up. Having been born and raised in Papua New Guinea (PNG), it was what I knew as home. But to me it became much more than home; it was where I learned what the Bahá'í Faith was and the spirit, love and purpose of this unifying, most recent world religion.

I grew up in a family where my parents' whole lives were dedicated to an incredible love that had grown within their very souls. Everything they did seemed to revolve around their love for the Bahá'í Faith and the spirit of service which it undoubtedly instilled within them. I saw a love and dedication to any and all kinds of development projects that would build up this country, which, although already spiritually rich, lagged in the basic training of education, health and social services and in the development and advancement of women and mothers, as well as the basic skills that so many of us take for granted.

My parents' service and dedication under these conditions provided me with a unique example from which I was able, in my own way, to learn and to which I could aspire on my path of becoming a Bahá'í. Incredible and inspiring as my parents were, I was also privileged to feel and see the spirit of the teachings of the Bahá'í Faith in Papua New Guinea. We lived in a province where I saw village after village embrace the Faith. This was an area where people truly had the most amazing spirit, reverence and depth of love for the Faith that surpassed all other loves. Their lives were simple, their souls untouched by the dross of this materialistic world, and they saw the power of this religion to unite them, one and all, regardless of tribe, traditional or cultural backgrounds or religious beliefs, which seemed for the most part to distinguish and divide in one way or another. With that said, one should understand that Papua New Guinea is a country with a population of about 5.5 million and more than 800 different cultures and languages.

As a child I grew up in a little town where there was one street with a couple of shops and a market with local produce. I often spent my holidays taking a flight into a mountainous area and spending weeks at a time in an area known as Daga. Daga is an area in PNG where there are thousands of Bahá'ís, so many that you could walk for days up and down mountains on paths along the edge of life-threatening cliffs, and through rivers and creeks, and you would come across village after village in which everyone had embraced the Bahá'í Faith and which echoed the greeting of Alláh-u-Abhá – God is Most Glorious. These were villages where there was no running water, no electricity, no paved roads or cars and where the houses were built out of village material using not a single nail. This area was materially so poor – they had few schools and health facilities – yet they possessed the greatest wealth spiritually. They were the happiest, most humble and most loving souls I have ever met. These people, in their love and simplicity, taught me what being a Bahá'í truly is. I loved being in this environment and surrounded by these people. I spent any holiday I could in this area, washing in the river, carrying pots of water on my head from the river to the village top where all the houses were, cooking our food on fire and sleeping on bamboo floors with as little as our sleeping bags or bed sheets. I came to have multiple parents who watched over me as if I were their own daughter, along with my family of three brothers, and my family was forever expanding. My parents adopted kids over the years from this village area so that they could come live with us in town and have an opportunity at a better education. Most of these village kids, they were lucky if they received the level of education to pass the National Exam at grade six, which determined if they could go on to high school. Bringing them into the town not only gave them exposure to what seemed like the world and was often a shock, but gave them the advantage of being in a school system where the percentage of those passing the National Exams was much higher as a result of more well-trained and consistent teachers.

In 1992 the Most Holy Book of the Bahá'í Faith was published in English. The Bahá'í communities in Daga area, unlike many communities worldwide which received their Most Holy Book in the mail and added it to their bookshelves, had the most dignified and reverent reception of it. Many communities, for months in advance, built Bahá'í centres or added new rooms to the ones they had already built so that this book, once received, would have a sacred and distinguished location. The members of the Bahá'í communities, many of which had to travel for days on foot to meet, met at one central location where international visitors also gathered to witness the celebrations and festivities that accompanied the anticipated arrival of the Most Holy Book. Traditional festivities took place over several days as their way of expressing their gratitude and praise on such an occasion. There was traditional dancing, with women dressed in grass skirts and men in traditional tapa cloths as they all danced to the sound of the beating Kundu drums. They harvested food from gardens and cooked feasts, often killing pigs, which are prized possessions and a sign of wealth, and roasting them in the ground under hot stones. But what was most humbling was the way in which these communities received and transported the Most Holy Book back to their villages. They had built beautiful boxes to hold the book. The boxes usually sat on carrying planks similar to a stretcher, which several people took turns carrying as they made the journey back up mountains, valleys and through rivers to return to their own villages.

As a child growing up I remember many festive occasions similar to this one, although with different causes. I remember walking a lot and often being told we were almost at our destination – of course, 'almost' to the local people but for us it was still eight hours of hiking. Many times we were hiking trails on which if our foot slipped or we staggered in the least we would be rolling down cliffs to our life's end. Of course, as children – and even to this day – we were always accompanied by quick and steady souls who on several occasions had to catch us before we fell over cliffs or were swept away by strong river currents. I remember during one long and difficult journey being lifted up and carried for hours on the shoulders of an inspirational figure in my life. Being shoulders above everyone else was like soaring through clouds, at least for me. To this day I never hear the end of it because, although I was young at the time, I was not that light! Although we recall those days vividly we also now laugh at how the time has come for the roles to be reversed, especially since the person who carried me now has Parkinson's and cannot walk those mountains like he used to.

These are the people and events that touched my soul and left memories I will never forget. They are the things that inspired me to be a Bahá'í, to strive to serve mankind and share with the world this uniting and healing message Bahá'u'lláh has brought. The power of the Bahá'í Faith not only brought together and unified villages and people within PNG but, to my continued amazement, I have seen the same influence of the uniting power of this world religion while on my travels across continents. It has made the world a family, uniting together those from different countries, cultures, creeds and religions. It has for certain made me feel at home wherever I have travelled and made me feel a part of a greater cause and a much greater family.

I feel I have been blessed through my life experiences and particularly by growing up in PNG. Of course, growing up in a Bahá'í home we were encouraged to learn about all the world religions. As a part of elementary school we had religious instruction classes once a week and for a long time I went to the Christian classes, which consisted of great stories and songs, although because I was not a Christian myself it was believed that I was for sure going to hell. This lack of acceptance, because I did not identify myself with a particular Christian denomination, did not seem to stop me from going to church. On occasion I went with friends or family, and even though there was a wonderful spirit of praise and gratitude, for me it seemed too ritualistic. I could not stand being preached to by some man who thought he had a greater or more spiritual connection to God than those in the audience. Of course I understand that there was once, partly due to illiteracy, a great need for the services of clergy and for them to share with the community the knowledge they acquired through absolute dedication to God. For me, I needed to feel a part of a community in which I could share and voice my thoughts and suggestions just as much as anyone else could, regardless of age, experience or wisdom.

The abolition of clergy and the teaching regarding the independent investigation for truth were things I really embraced about the Bahá'í Faith. They were something that really attracted me and gave me a sense of welcomed responsibility, as well as a sense that I was part of a greater community. I had a role even as a child and youth and now as a maturing adult. I also loved that, unlike other religions, the Bahá'í Faith not only tolerated other religions but accepted them and embraced them as part of one divine plan. They are all religions that have come from the same source – God – and although they may have different social teachings, their core spiritual teachings are the same.

For me it seemed religion should be a way of life and not just something I decide I would commit to for a couple hours here or there, like on Sunday morning when I went to church. To me the Bahá'í Faith has answers and offers practical solutions to the world's problems. It aims to unite, to rise above all barriers of separation in one form or the other; it gives me a sense of purpose and in some mysterious way provided a light at the end of what many times seemed like a long, dark, lonely tunnel.

Being a Bahá'í and having grown up in PNG I had a great sense of appreciation for life and the opportunities that I was given. I went to Canada for high school and felt lucky to be able to go to a small international Bahá'í school. Although moving to North America brought with it many tests and difficulties, I seem to have been a little protected in a loving Bahá'í environment where many youth with international backgrounds were experiencing similar cultural differences. In this environment I faced tests and difficulties, most often in the form of individuals and their lack of appreciation for life and what it offered, perhaps because I felt that so much of what we had were things that in some parts of the world were so hard to come by. However, through it all, school was more than just some place where we learned. We matured into these service-orientated, young world citizens; we became a family that loved and supported each other; and, more sacred than anything, we established relationships that will last a lifetime.

I was inspired to leave this protected environment at the beginning of my senior year in high school. I felt I could somehow or other get into university when I was ready to go. I wanted to go to South America and serve in some capacity. I wanted to give a piece of me back to the world, to share my life and learn something from 'the real world', as many would put it. My parents were hesitant about the idea but lovingly encouraged and supported me to follow my heart's calling; my academic advisors, on the other hand, were quite concerned and discouraging for, after all, what university would accept a high school drop out?

My heart was set on going to help in an orphanage in Honduras when shortly before I was to leave, there was a huge, devastating storm in Central America. This halted all communication between me and the orphanage and so I was made to look into other options. I ended up going to Ecuador and having the most amazing time. Of course, it also was accompanied by its own range of challenges. I was thrown into an environment in which I could hardly speak the language – you learn fast when no one speaks English – and I had little communication with my friends and family. While in Ecuador I met many other inspirational Baháʼí youth with whom I travelled the country and lived in small, remote areas. We offered our services in any capacity we could. We held children's classes focused on spiritual and moral character building, devotional meetings and literacy classes for women and girls. We volunteered at local health clinics, giving babies and children their regular health checkups and vaccinations. It was a wonderful experience that brought with it challenges. Of course the most distinguished memories are those that had spiritual rewards, rewards of seeing a radiant smile on the face of a child and a mother's pride as she read to her children. There are also memories of walking right into the middle of a riot where we heard piercing gunshots and saw tear-gas being fired right at us and we turned and ran for our lives. These were thrilling moments which we look back upon with fondness and most of all gratitude that we were again so well protected from harm.

I took two years off school and after Ecuador went to Guyana and Mexico before I decided to go to university. I was blessed to go on a nine day pilgrimage with my family during this time and it was an experience that only strengthened my love for this incredible Faith, which right from infancy I had already seen making inspiring changes in the world.

These were all experiences that strengthened my love for Baháʼuʼlláh and the Baháʼí Faith. As life took its course the Faith became something that was not only precious to my parents but became my own. It is through the Baháʼí Faith that I feel my life has been, and continues to be, blessed with the most incredible experiences, opportunities and people, people who have become my family because of a shared love and vision. The Baháʼí Faith is what continues to give my life meaning and hope in all the surrounding despair, calamity and war, and I just pray that I will continually be able to offer back to the world of humanity what it has given to me.

A WARM PLACE IN MY HEART

Omid Khorramian

Omid Khorramian grew up in a Bahá'í family in Peru. His mother is Peruvian and his father has been an Iranian pioneer in Peru since 1981. Omid was 17 years old when he wrote this and was studying Business Administration at the National University in Piura, Peru. He wrote in English, which is his second language.

Preamble

If you want to study at University in Peru, you have two options: the first one is to study in a private university, which is very expensive. The other option is to study at a national university, where you don't pay any money; they have more prestige around the world than private universities. In order to study at a national university you must take a very difficult test for which thousands of students study for several months to pass. Very few students are received at each branch.

Story

During the first days of this year, after finishing school, I had to study for the entrance test for the National University in Piura. But at the same time there was going to be, in Lima, Peru's capital, a very important course for my Bahá'í life. This course, which was to take 20 days, was designed to develop an excellent character in each participant and to prepare participants for real community service.

I had to decide what option to choose: studying to take my test or taking this Bahá'í course which was also very important to me. I thought about it for more than two weeks. I was praying a lot during that time that Bahá'u'lláh would help me choose the best option and I decided to take the course. After the course, I was going to study very hard for my test. I went on the course and after the 20 days I went back home, now more enthusiastic than before, to continue with my pre-youth group and two children's classes.

April came and I had to study to be ready to take the test and go to the National University in Piura. I used to study from Monday to Friday, morning, afternoon and night. My Saturdays were dedicated to my pre-youth group and children's classes.

One night a Bahá'í friend called me from a small city, Negritos. It's about three hours from my house. In this place there is a small community with ten Bahá'ís. He called me to ask for help. The Negritos Bahá'í community wanted to begin a children's class but they didn't have any experience with such classes and they didn't know how to get them started. He asked me to go there every weekend, get a children's class started and work with them until they felt ready to continue with the children on their own.

So I accepted to help them. From Monday to Friday I used to study. On Saturdays I worked with my pre-youth and children's classes and as soon as I finished my classes with the youngsters I travelled to Negritos until Sunday night and sometimes until Monday afternoon. I had lot of faith that at the moment I had to take the test Bahá'u'lláh was going to open my mind and that I was going to go to the university.

The day to take the test came! My teachers told me: 'We know the effort you have made but we think you aren't going to go to university because thousands of students are going to take this test and they have been studying for it for years.' So l answered them, 'Let's wait for the results.' I had confidence that I would succeed at the test and go to university. During the test I prayed a lot. Happily I finished one hour before the other students.

The moment arrived to see the test results and all my friends and teachers were surprised that I passed the entrance exam for university in second place for my branch. I wasn't surprised because I knew that Bahá'u'lláh was with me all the time. I was so happy and thankful.

So we can see that a person with faith in God and with effort can achieve all his/her goals and God will fill that person with innumerable blessings.

Faith means unconditional belief and total confidence. The sacred writings exhort us to have confidence in God. This unconditional confidence can be achieved by a personal spiritual experience, by reading the sacred writings, praying and meditating. I close with this quotation from the words of Bahá'u'lláh:

The essence of faith is fewness of words and abundance of deeds;

he whose words exceed his deeds, know verily his death is better than his life. (Bahá'u'lláh, *Tablets*, p. 156)

Compiler's note: After sending this story, Omid followed up by sharing, several weeks later, this account of his involvement in one of the many Bahá'í Dance Workshops that take place around the world:

The Workshop is a group of young people who meet to learn and practice dances. The dances are very special because they show social problems like drug addiction, inequality and more. We use these dances to show the pain people are suffering because of these social problems and we give them an alternative to change that pain into happiness.

Two years ago, at the end of December, there was going to be a project in Ica. This place is far from my house. The project was organized by a dance group from Canada, 'Generation of Hope'. The project was going to take 12 days and many youth from Ecuador and Peru were invited to attend.

At that time I wanted to create a Workshop and start to practise with them but I didn't know the dances, so I decided to go on the project and learn them.

On the project we had lots of beautiful moments. We learned a lot about discipline, how to get a Workshop started, how to direct it, how to give excellent presentations and other related things.

Afterwards I went back to my community. I was so excited to get a Workshop started! I wanted to get youth to start the Workshop so I talked with Bahá'í youth about starting it with them. They were excited to start it too. We practised with the group for almost seven months.

We had to stop when I had to take a Bahá'í course that was very important to me, the 'Bahá'í lifelong service course'. After the course I had to study to pass my university entrance test. I promised myself: 'Omid, you are going to study hard and will pass that test and after that you will get a new Workshop started and not just with Bahá'ís.'

I studied hard in the little time that I had. The moment arrived for me to take the test and, fortunately, as previously mentioned, I passed the test.

Now the second step was to get people, especially those who were not Bahá'ís, to start the dance group. I prayed a lot to Bahá'u'lláh to help me find people. It was so difficult it took almost a month to find individuals who wanted to belong to a dance group.

One day I went to a meeting just of young people to get information about different careers that the university offered. I don't know how but I saw five people there that I had never seen before so I decided to talk to them about the Bahá'í Faith. They liked it a lot. After that I explained to them that I wanted to get a dance group going and I was looking for people who wanted to belong to the group. They were so excited with the idea that I started the performances with them. Little by little, more friends came, bringing with them more and more people. We are 15 now, none Bahá'ís except my two sisters and me.

Our performances are from 4 p.m. to 7 p.m. We have been having these performances for almost a month.

We recently got a name for the group: Breaking Barriers.

We are planning that when we are ready, when we know all the dances, we are going to have lots of presentations at schools, universities, parks, on television and in our main presentation area, theatres.

I am so happy to get this dance group going. They are so good, these guys. I like their way of thinking. I know that we are going to do many things with this group. I know that Bahá'u'lláh helped me to get this group together.

José Silva

Introduction and translation by Regan Roy

José Silva Nuñez was 16 years old in 2006 when he wrote his contribution. He lives in the District of Cieneguilla on the outskirts of Lima, Peru's capital city. José, his parents and his sister, Michelle, joined the Bahá'í community several years ago. José is a Grade 10 student at the local Waldorf school. He is a gifted musician, playing classical guitar, and he also loves singing. He teaches several children's classes, one at a local orphanage, and he also facilitates a pre-youth group and a youth group at home on the weekends.

A Story without End

I'm a Grade 10 student at the local Waldorf school, and in my class there are just 15 students, so it's pretty small. During class breaks I take out my guitar and start singing some Bahá'í songs. Some of my classmates go outside or eat something and others hang out and listen to me, trying to sing along. My class is different from others in the school because we are quite musically inclined and have pretty good voices! Anyway, it so happens that the most musically talented are also those most interested in learning the Bahá'í songs, asking me the words of the songs, especially one called 'The Light of Unity', which includes the quotation, 'So powerful is the light of unity that it can illuminate the whole earth.' (Bahá'u'lláh, *Gleanings*, p. 288)

The whole school likes this song and it reached the ears of our music tutor. It was getting close to our semester 'fiesta' in which each classroom has to make a presentation to the whole school, including the parents. The tutor asked me to teach this song to everybody in my class during music classes until finally they all learned it, practising it first thing every morning. Just imagine, a whole classroom singing at the top of their lungs, together, words of Bahá'u'lláh. It was just too exciting. Every day, morning and afternoon, you could hear this melody all around and even a block away from the school you could hear the song clearly.

So several days before the presentation I took the opportunity to call up a Bahá'í friend named Carlos Medina, who has an amazing voice and was the one who taught me the song. Carlos has sung this same song on radio and television in Venezuela, Peru and Chile. I invited him to come to my school on the day of the presentation (15 July), only telling him that he should come and that he would hear a surprise.

Finally the big day arrived. In the auditorium in front of a crowd of between 200 and 300, the tenth grade (the one in which I study) began its presentation. First we played several folk songs and, finally, 'The Light of Unity'. Oh, by the way, in his introduction the music tutor said, 'We will continue with a song that I feel has truly united our class and is our favourite song, and we hope you enjoy it.' And we started singing . . .

In the audience were members of the local Bahá'í community of Cieneguilla, from which there are nine children who study in different grades at the school. It was spectacular, like a birthday present sent by God, and almost half of the auditorium started to sing the chorus (the quotation) along with us. It was unforgettable.

But Carlos didn't show up. Finally, about ten minutes after the presentation ended, he arrived. It seems that work and slow public transport were the problem but, well, better late than never and in the end, things happen for a reason.

I had spoken a lot to my music teacher about Carlos, so after the presentation we got together for a special meeting with him. It was like a fireside with our whole class. We sang 'The Light of Unity' once more and Carlos was really impressed that everybody knew the words of the song. Then we sang some other Bahá'í songs and after this all the gang were really enthusiastic and motivated to do something together with the Bahá'ís. So I thought about this situation and decided not to waste the opportunity to channel this energy and drive. All of this created the idea to organize a get-together for youth over one whole weekend. This was the result of singing this great song.

Later, José sent this addition:

You remember the guys who sang the Bahá'í song together with me during a presentation at my school? Well, seeing and feeling their motivation, it occurred to me to organize a get-together for youth. The main reason is as follows. My home community of Cieneguilla is very new to the Faith and there aren't very many Bahá'ís so far (especially youth). In fact, I am the only Bahá'í youth at the moment who facilitates any activities, so I would love it if more youth were able to feel the pleasure of serving the Cause of God.

The get-together consisted of a series of workshops on topics like backbiting, youth, personal conduct, and so on, and the final topic was the first chapter of Ruhi book 1. The meetings took place over two days and about 20 young people attended. Two families grasped the real significance of these meetings and my main objective now is that they become deepened and attend other community activities. Anyway, these two families are the Reateguis family (Jefferson and Lizeth) and the Díaz family (Gary, Carlos, Hermila, Ethel and Christian). These are the youth I was looking and longing for, for a long, long time. Right now they are studying Ruhi book 5 and they are all very active. Just last week we sang together at our regional Bahá'í convention in Lima and were very well received by the community.

As you can see, the story is never ending . . .

Edward Robertson

Edward Robertson grew up in Swift Current in southern Saskatchewan, Canada, the son of a Canadian father and Iranian mother. His family farms near Zealandia, Saskatchewan. He has a brother, Navid, and a sister, Tahirih. After graduating from high school, he offered to serve at the Bahá'í World Centre in Haifa, Israel, and shared some of his journal entries from that period. He begins his contribution with some quotations chosen from the Bahá'í writings.

> Anas, son of Málik – may God be pleased with him – hath said: 'The Apostle of God – may the blessings of God and His salutations be upon Him – hath said: "By the shore of the sea is a city, suspended beneath the Throne, and named 'Akká. He that dwelleth therein, firm and expecting a reward from God – exalted be He – God will write down for him, until the Day of Resurrection, the recompense of such as have been patient, and have stood up, and knelt down, and prostrated themselves, before Him."' (Bahá'u'lláh, *Epistle*, pp. 178–9).

I bring you tidings of a city betwixt two mountains in Syria, in the middle of a meadow, which is called 'Akká. Verily, he that entereth therein, longing for it and eager to visit it, God will forgive his sins, both of the past and of the future. (ibid. p. 178)

It is called 'Akká. He that hath been bitten by one of its fleas is better, in the estimation of God, than he who hath received a grievous blow in the path of God. And he that raiseth therein the call to prayer, his voice will be lifted up unto Paradise. (ibid. p. 179)

13 June

Well, I've moved again today. Say goodbye to Haifa and welcome to 'Akká! I'll be living in the Old City, directly beside the House of 'Abbúd. It's such a blessing to live here. Just next door to where Bahá'u'lláh revealed the Kitáb-i-Aqdas. This place is exactly how an Arabian city would be portrayed in the movies. Everything here reminds me of Aladdin. If you flew over 'Akká you would see the numerous minarets standing tall so you could see where every mosque in town was, the thick stone wall surrounding the entire city and even the rooftops of the Houses of 'Abbúd and 'Abdu'lláh Páshá. From the sea you could see the beautiful harbour full of old boats, waves crashing against the stone wall which surrounds the city and the dozens of men fishing for their daily catch.

My view is always from the ground. Every building looks like a mansion. Each one is a towering two, even three or four storeys high. Streets are no longer common – just narrow and winding stone paths meant for horses and people on foot. Through the middle of town is the bazaar, the central shopping area. Of course it has its plain old shops for clothes, CDs and souvenirs but there is always something a little different there than from any market at home. This place has enough interesting smells to drive a dog crazy. Walking through the bazaar the first smell you find is the fruity scent of locals smoking water pipes. From there you pass by the sweet-scented perfume shops, then the airconditioned fruit stands, the bakeries where you get pitta straight from the oven, the fish market with an unforgivable odour, only to finish off smelling fresh falafel and kebab.

The experience I will never forget is watching the sun set across the Mediterranean Sea. When going to watch the sunset I always have to find my way to the top of the 15 foot sea wall. Some days it is as simple as stairs, and others as difficult as a vertical climb but it is worth the struggle every time. To see the waves rushing in, the fishermen standing out in the water or the ships on their way home before dark, all of this on an endless sea with the fattest orange sun in the background. Day after day, my evenings are spent sitting atop this wall watching, praying and meditating. This is a fairly common part of my day with the sea wall just outside my front door.

Every house in the city somehow manages to be unique. My house was similar to every house in town only in the sense that it is made of thick stone walls and has cockroach problems. Many people have big homes. Some live above restaurants or shops. A lucky few have houses built into the sea wall and have windows facing straight into the sea. I can only imagine the noise from the waves. Our place is small but, thankfully, on the ground floor. You first enter a newly renovated common area but everything becomes older as you venture into the house. My bedroom is at the end of the house. 'The Cave' is its nickname. Being so close to the sea, there is a lot of humidity. It just happens that all of it would settle into one room of the house. When you look around you see the curve above every entrance, the rough stone walls and the high domed ceiling. Every morning you wake up to kids playing in the street and Arabic music playing.

16 June

What a place! The culture really is completely different here from Haifa. It's strange because everyone here is living their regular lives in this sacred place where Bahá'u'lláh stayed for nine years. We've been watching World Cup soccer just down the street, buying our bread and fruit in the bazaar, sitting on the city walls, all sorts of things. One neat thing is that around the prison there is a moat. It's mostly kept unclean and full of garbage except for one small section. This small section happens to have basketball courts and soccer fields. This is where we do our sporting fun. Often we play games with the locals.

I've been having lots of time to think about what I'm doing here. Coming from a small farming town and ending up in Israel is a big change. Home was full of wide open spaces, with fields of golden wheat beyond eyes' sight. The clouded skies came alive and were impressive day after day. Everything was quiet, peaceful and relaxing. The grass was soft and green and the air was clean and dry.

The food has changed, my friends have changed, my family is left behind and a whole new life begins. These are just little things that have changed. They are just small insignificant aspects of home that are given up and sacrificed for something greater. They are given up for a greater purpose and a greater Cause than me and my own life. All that I have now is my life and my time. What better thing is there to do in my youth than to share this with the whole world? In the end, when I return home, I'll have lost nothing and have only gained from this experience. I gain life skills, wisdom and a whole new lookout on life. It's an opportunity of a lifetime. There's not a second to waste.

Spring 2007

After my year of service at the Bahá'í World Centre was complete, I went straight to French Guiana for four months of pioneering. I had no idea what to expect and it was all definitely a surprise. I share a small house with another Bahá'í. We live in a tropical forest. We have electricity but no running water. So life is a little different from Canada.

Nonetheless I'm enjoying my service here very much. There are lots of Bahá'ís here, so I'm not teaching particularly but keeping everyone active. My days are spent working mostly with children and youth. I do three children's classes, three pre-youth classes and two study circles, so I'm busy enough keeping in contact with hundreds of young Bahá'ís every week.

The people here are very spiritual and kind people. Everyone really loves the Bahá'ís. One of the difficulties is that although everyone thinks highly of the Bahá'ís, nobody knows much about us. Even some of the Bahá'ís know very little. Most of the adults do not speak French but the local language of Taki Taki, so it's difficult to deepen them. This is why I work with the youth and hopefully they can carry on some marvellous work as they get older.

So that's it in a nutshell. I'm very happy here. The service is going very well. I can't see myself doing much else with my life right now. There's so much the youth can do to help the Bahá'í communities around the world. This period of service is definitely filled with tests but it's all there to help me grow. The experience we gain from a youth year of service gives us qualities and skills that we can use for the rest of lives. I have three more months in French Guiana and I pray that this short period of my life can help move the world.

Sylvain Hutchison

Sylvain Hutchison is the son of a British father and French mother who met, married and moved to Africa to pioneer for the Bahá'í Faith. Sylvain thus began his international experiences early. He now resides in Canada.

My Experience as a Young Bahá'í

I would like to write about my experiences and the thoughts that have accompanied me throughout my travels around the world because travelling has become the passion of my life. It's all about exploring new countries, cities, places, understanding others' culture, different lifestyles, different mentalities. You get to meet people from totally different backgrounds, different educations, yet you communicate with the same language and you realize that we are not all that different from each other. It is such an enlightening experience, a real eye opener in a world that is infinitely big, yet surprisingly small. It made me realize: isn't this what the writings are all about, getting to know our neighbours so that we can accept our differences and all live together, peacefully and united? How can we live in such a world if we do not make an effort to get to know each other and accept one another?

Here are a couple of Bahá'í experiences that I would like to share with you. Sydney, Australia: no, not the capital city, but big and famous, yes. I got to the youth hostel late at night, tired, not knowing anyone there and not knowing what I wanted to see and visit. I took a look at the pamphlets they had near the kitchen and in the middle of them was one about the Bahá'í temple! It hit me, of course. How could I have forgotten? I read up on it beforehand but had completely forgotten about it for some reason. It was one of those last minute trips. This is where I have to say thanks to Sydney's Local Spiritual Assembly. Later on I would realize that they have the pamphlets everywhere – at the train station, airport – very impressive, and it worked, I'm living proof!

So I decided to go to the temple the next morning. I finally made it after two or three hours. It was just breathtaking, standing there in front of a beautiful scenic garden. It was the first time I have ever been to a Bahá'í temple. It was very exciting for me. I walked inside the little office on the corner and, of course, I met a retired Canadian couple who had come to visit their son. What a small world. Could I have gone any farther than Australia from Canada?

I then walked inside the temple, sat in a chair dead in the middle of it, took up a prayer book and read a prayer. Above me on the ceiling was the Greatest Name, the nine openings all around me, and not a single sound could be heard from the centre of the temple. This was surprising because it's close to a busy road and all the doors and windows were open. I can't describe the feeling I had when I entered; it was magical. It took me another few hours to get back to Sydney and what a pleasant and satisfying little day trip I had. It's the kind of experience that just has to be lived to be understood. No words are great enough to explain it all.

Another experience I would like to share is one that happened over the course of several months when I lived in Malaysia. I had contacted the Canadian National Spiritual Assembly and it gave me names that I could reach in Malaysia. I tried to contact them but didn't get a reply at the very beginning, I was wondering if there were any Bahá'ís on this little island I was living on. It had less than a half a million population, mostly in the capital city, and I lived half an hour away.

One day while driving through the city I saw this blue sign with 'Bahá'í' written on it. I bounced up and looked back from the back seat of my friend's car. I couldn't believe my eyes. My friend thought I had seen a ghost. Well, that confirmed the presence of Bahá'ís on the island and, fair enough, I got a reply in the weeks to come. I was told that there were so many Bahá'ís on this little island that they had four Local Spiritual Assemblies – truly unbelievable! So I went to the 19 Day Feasts and was even invited to a wedding, met very kind people and it was just fantastic. I went into people's little homes where we had our feasts, and when it came time to eat, we were sitting on the floor, with rice and chicken in our plates eating with our hands, while someone was playing the guitar and singing songs. It was so different from our feasts back home but somehow I felt so close to them. They reminded me of the type of feasts we used to have in Africa where my parents were pioneers for quite some time. I was only a little boy but grew up there and have fond memories of it all. Well, it gets even better. They have a song book, just like in Africa, and believe it or not, some songs were the exact same ones we used to sing in Africa, just in a different language! Africa and Asia – can there be any places more different? Yet once again I found common ground.

The last experience happened in Barcelona, Spain, where I stayed for one night. I walked into the youth hostel and met a Frenchman and an Englishman. It was great for me, as I could speak both languages, but the Englishman couldn't speak French and the Frenchman couldn't speak English. Well, I didn't have to translate a single word because the Englishman knew a bit of Spanish from his dad who was Spanish, the Frenchman and I had studied Spanish at school, so we all communicated in Spanish. Though our Spanish was really not that good, it was good enough to understand each other and to communicate on a basic level. That was the highlight of the trip. I still have a smile on my face when I think of it – those couple of hours were an amazing experience for me. It made me think of the international language that the Bahá'í writings talk about. Spanish wasn't the native language of any of us, we all had to learn it, yet it was the only language we could all communicate in. This doesn't happen every day.

No matter where you go in this world, being a Bahá'í is like being part of a huge but close family and even if you don't know a single soul in the country you are visiting, you can be sure that the Bahá'ís will welcome you with open arms. My message is this: travelling brings people together, makes people understand each other and opens our eyes to a totally new dimension, one that has peace and unity written all over its long and winding road.

Jesse Harris

Jesse Harris was born 2 March 1988 and is from Arnprior, Ontario, Canada. At the time of writing, he is living in Takamatsu, Kagawa Prefecture, Japan and is hoping to go to university to study science and, later, medicine.

A Simple Question

I can recall a time in my life, vaguely, when somebody in a conversation about the Bahá'í Faith asked me, 'Why are you a Bahá'í?' This question was asked in passing, really quite simply put and not clearly aimed. I probably answered it just as simply, something along the lines of 'I believe that Bahá'u'lláh was right', which is not really an answer. When I received this question in my email account I was at first struck at the simplicity of the question, five words long, 15 letters, one apostrophe and one question mark. It then occurred to me that this question had far-reaching implications which touched the very root of my personal faith. I then realized that I didn't know how to answer, which worried me at first. It is not that simple really: what was the real reason I became a Bahá'í? What is the principal factor behind my beliefs?

There are people within the Bahá'í community who would be able to point to a specific time in their life and say, 'That is it', in the sense that they can locate a time, place and situation that inspired them to be a Bahá'í. Some can also indicate one key truth or central concept, in their mind, in the theology of the Faith or in the universe in general that led them specifically to the Bahá'í community. For many of us, though, the question is not so black and white. Of course, for all of the people mentioned above, or anyone who considers himself a Bahá'í for that matter, there are probably many things working in the background that inspired them to commit to the Cause but some can name the key factors in their faith more than others. Personally, I have tossed this question over in my brain a lot of times and as yet have arrived at little in the way of a solid answer. This is not to say that I don't have great faith in the teachings or that I don't really consider myself a Bahá'í but rather that I cannot figure out what, specifically, made me become one. What produced my faith? What event inspired me to sign my card and continue with the Cause? Why am I a Bahá'í?

I think it came down to a whole slew of factors, none of them recognizably bigger than any of the others but all significant in their own way. When I turned 15 I signed my card the first chance I got. This was not only because I wanted to be a Bahá'í that moment but also because my birthday is on 2 March, the very first day of the fast. I had actually been looking forward to the prospect of fasting for years, and wanted to participate in it very badly, so I signed my card at something like 6 a.m., followed this with fast breakfast with my mother and then headed back to my bed so I could be at least partly awake for school. Before this time I had already studied Ruhi books 1 to 4, finishing my first book 1 on my twelfth birthday. This goes to show that I had a strong Bahá'í identity before I turned 15 or had the option of signing my card. Although it is good that I had Bahá'í beliefs ingrained in me long before the age of maturity,[4] it adds to the difficulty of this question because the events leading up to me signing my card have very little relevance as to *why* I signed it. People who grow up in non-Bahá'í families have that advantage, I suppose, that they can recall the date of their declaration as the day they became a believer, while for someone like me it becomes a little more confusing as to what was the deciding moment.

I have long known and believed in the logical proofs of the

---

4 Bahá'u'lláh designates 15 as the age of maturity for people to commence their own spiritual decision-making, i.e. with fasting, etc.

Faith. I look at different aspects of each of them and it becomes clear to me that it only makes sense to believe in God and therefore to believe in Bahá'u'lláh's teachings. Reading different passages by 'Abdu'l-Bahá or just meditating on the various aspects of the Faith makes it very clear to me that being a Bahá'í is the right thing for me. Although these things are obvious to me, I don't feel that this has much specific relevance to the question of why I decided to join the Faith. I knew of them at the time when I signed my card as well but they were largely beside the point. Knowing something is often a lot different from believing in something.

I briefly stated that my mother is a Bahá'í when I mentioned my first fast breakfast. This implies that my family is, at least partially, Bahá'í. This is true: my mother is Bahá'í and her mother and various cousins and uncles and such on that side of the family are as well. On my father's side of the family I am the only Bahá'í. I have an older brother and a younger sister, neither of whom signed their card on their fifteenth birthday or since. This shows that although I was introduced to the Faith by my family, it is not really why I am a Bahá'í. I'm sure everyone knows some Bahá'ís who grew up in a rich spiritual background and their personal faith flourished as a result. This was not quite the case in my family. My own personal belief in Bahá'u'lláh was established through my own personal investigation of things and not necessarily because of my Bahá'í lineage. This is not to say that my mother did not give me children's classes or that I was completely on my own in the discovery of my faith but it does mean that this was probably not the key factor in my decision.

I will say, though, that I fell in love with the Bahá'í Faith at a very young age. Any chance I got I would try and spend time with the Bahá'ís, joining summer camp, and Ruhi circles at a younger than normal age. I can even remember when I was quite young, always wanting to get dressed up for feast nights and always looking forward to anything that was happening at my house regarding the Bahá'í Faith. Of course, as I grew up I started going to junior youth/youth events, which gave me a sense of community I felt nowhere else but was very typical of Bahá'í youth life. The area where I lived had nothing of a Bahá'í youth community; I was really the only one for many years, so I often went to great lengths to gather up people from all around in order to get to the Bahá'í youth gatherings. I lived outside Ottawa, Canada, in a small town by the name of Arnprior, where we always had to stretch a bit to get the nine people for the Local Spiritual Assembly. Going to those youth events, though, often travelling hours to get there or having to work and organize for hours to get them to come to my house, always paid off with amazing experiences. All of this led to my great love for the Bahá'í community, which gave me the desire to truly proclaim my devotion to it by becoming a Bahá'í myself.

One thing that is important to mention, though, is that I did not sign my card for the community alone. I have encountered people in my years of being a Bahá'í who at one point in their lives were not able to distinguish the Bahá'í community from the Bahá'í Faith. These people tend to become very disillusioned if at some point in their lives they are living in an area where there is no community or if a local community fails them in some way. At this point they encounter this issue: if the Bahá'í Faith = the Bahá'í community and the Bahá'í community = undependable, does that mean that the Bahá'í Faith = undependable? Growing up in an area without much of a Bahá'í community dispelled this myth and allowed my love of the Bahá'í Faith and the community to grow together but still allowed them to be distinguishable from one another. My love for my religion is linked to the beauty of the central principles, the power of the Cause, the glory of the central figures and, as I have seen in so many people, like myself, the personal changes it facilitates. These things are really hard to pin down and it is really hard to explain how, why or when these influenced my faith. I do know, though, that these are hugely influential in my life.

This is the best that I can do to explain my personal faith in the sense of why I chose to become a Bahá'í or how my early belief in Bahá'u'lláh developed. This may be vague, fragmented and unclear but it is, largely, the best I can do. This is really an answer to why did I become a Bahá'í but this does not answer why I am still a Bahá'í. Things change, ideas grow and mature. Experience and time will do a lot to a person. So, at age 18, for myself, I ask, Why am I still a Bahá'í?

To answer this question I will start by explaining where I am and what I am doing. Currently I am in Takamatsu, Japan, giving a year of service to the Bahá'í community here. I have been in this country for about three months at the time of writing. In the time I have been in Japan I have learned more about myself than I will ever be able to explain. I have done things, experienced life and lived in a way that almost no one of my age will be able to. I have gained an amazing set of skills and traits throughout my days of being a Bahá'í, especially while here, many of which huge numbers of people never acquire, especially by age 18. To name just a few, I have learned to think spiritually, creatively and dynamically, my personal skills have greatly prospered through this time, I have acquired knowledge of the nature of the world, my leadership and organizational skills have flourished and I have acquired a clearer personal identity, which helped me get through the awkward junior/early youth period. I cannot begin to properly name all the different situations that the Faith guided me away from for my own benefit. Looking back and reflecting, it is clear how great a service it did for me to have that set of rules for myself through my high school years, and although everyone seems to have an idea of what they should be doing, having the Bahá'í laws laid out so clearly really makes it much easier to do the right thing.

In my life, like the life of many other Bahá'ís, there have been a good number of small signs that seem to reaffirm my faith in weird ways. Just since I arrived in Japan I can think of many different things that have come up that make me thank God for His creative style and fantastic ability to answer prayers in a way that I would have never expected. I will review one example which I have been living in for the past while. In my life in Canada I was never required to learn how to clean. This is just how things worked out at my houses (my parents divorced when I was two). It was just not something that happened. My mother despised cleaning and felt it unfair to inflict this task on her children, so she hired a person to come over and clean, infrequently. My father, as an extreme opposite, really enjoyed keeping an immaculate house and didn't mind cleaning (as much as one can really not mind cleaning), so didn't teach his children, knowing that if we cleaned he would just have to do it again after us. The result was that as I left home I was without said skill set. Coming onto my year of service, I asked God to challenge me in a way that would allow for personal growth because I was quite interested in gaining something from this year away from my 'real life'. One of the results was that I was placed in a community where the best service I could render entailed me doing the vast majority of the housework for one family I was living with. I do not speak Japanese so I am highly limited in what I can do and there is a large amount of work that my host parents here do, so if they were forced to do their own housework, the Bahá'í activities that they participated in would be forced to come to a relatively grinding halt. So since I came here I have been forced to learn how to clean very quickly, and although it is something that I would have never thought would be a main component of my service, it is the perfect answer to my request to God. This is an isolated, relatively simple and easy to explain example of this sort of dynamic but such dynamics are present in my life in quite a lot of ways. This reinforces my faith every day; every time I think of this divine irony I am reminded of how powerful the Faith is in a lot of ways.

Another great inspiration of my personal faith at this point in my life are the spiritually illumined people I have encountered. It would almost be pointless to try to explain any of them very clearly or try and give you well illustrated examples. This is the sort of thing that you have to see and feel to understand. Sometimes I see the spark of the glory of the Faith in a small child, who has, already, begun to show signs of the fantastic spirituality that I have seen nowhere other than in the Bahá'í community. It may be that the child makes a comment that is far beyond his age or that his actions separate him so clearly from the majority of children of his age. This child is already becoming a Bahá'í in that sense. There are people I have encountered, my age, whose current level of spiritual greatness, coupled with their seemingly limitless potential, make them truly indescribable people. Some of these actually bring tears to my eyes occasionally, when I contemplate the spiritual victories they will bring about. There are also those seasoned Bahá'í champions, working in the various structures of the Faith, those living and working in Haifa or back in my home country of Canada or here in Japan. They are the ones who are currently the driving force of the institutions and who are responsible for the bulk of the work that is being done in any particular part of the world. There is also the group of Baháʼís that often goes unnoticed in many ways, from whom I actually get a lot of inspiration. I am tempted to say that there is almost nothing more inspiring than somebody in the last years of his life but still on fire with the love of Baháʼuʼlláh, willing to help in any way humanly possible, despite his physical difficulties. I can recall personal examples of all of these types in my own life and I'm sure that for many who are reading this faces and personages pop into their heads as I demonstrated each of those inspirational types. Whenever I am set in front of another example of any of these types of people my heart jumps for joy and my faith is rekindled.

This is, of course, not to mention the spiritual giants that have gone before us, those few souls of infinite value on whom the foundation of the Faith was built. This includes the Dawn-breakers and their spiritual descendants, the Martha Root and Agnes Alexander types, or my personal favourite, the great titan of Shoghi Effendi, whose epic work has left me in sheer awe. Whenever I hear of some small detail of their lives, which gives me a glimpse of their fantastic nature, I am always profoundly moved.

A final concept that grounds me quite firmly in the Faith is the glory of the central principles. I sometimes do the following: I think about the world, everything in it, the trends that are evolving (or devolving as it were), the things that are happening, the issues that are presenting and how everything is being managed. I look at everything; I really analyse the world from top to bottom, everything that is going on and what will probably happen next, but with the important exception of the Baháʼí Faith. Everything, without the community of Baháʼuʼlláh factoring into the picture, what does it look like? Pretty abysmal, is my opinion. I don't think I need to clearly demonstrate this much more than this: anyone beyond the age of twelve and with a television set would be able to name tons of problems in the world and it would not be easy for a Harvard professor to argue that they are improving.

Now look at the Bahá'í Faith and its context in the world. What is it doing, what patterns is it creating and what will happen to the world if its goals are realized? You see a world where the problems that once seemed so oppressive that they would swallow up the world, are now undone just as a matter of course. Think of the possibilities! Think of the prosperity! Think of the progress! Think of the communities, the government, the people, the life that we would all be living! In all my life the Bahá'í Faith is the only thing that offers this kind of hope, this deliverance from suffering and problems. This truly inspiring and amazingly realistic seeming world is only accomplished through Bahá'í principles, which begs the question, why would I not be a Bahá'í?

So all of these jumbled thoughts give the reasons why I am a Bahá'í and why I hope I will never leave the Faith. They also give the reason why I find myself across the world cleaning a Japanese house and why I am enjoying every minute of it. This is really the best that I think I will be able to do in order to explain my Faith to anyone. It is a hard thing to peg down. There are so many reasons and sometimes it is so hard to say where one ends and the next begins. I hope that in what I have written someone will find something inspirational, interesting or at least amusing in my answer. Even if no one does, I found it quite fascinating to think about. If you are a Bahá'í, I advise you ask yourself this question. The answer may be surprising. I know that mine was. Why are you a Bahá'í?

Bibliography

'Abdu'l-Bahá. *Paris Talks*. London: Baháí Publishing Trust, 1967.
— *The Promulgation of Universal Peace*. Wilmette, IL: Baháí Publishing Trust, 1982.
— *Selections from the Writings of 'Abdu'l-Bahá*. Haifa: Baháí World Centre, 1978.

Abdul Baha on Divine Philosophy. Boston: The Tudor Press, 1918.

Baháí Prayers: A Selection of Prayers revealed by Bahá'u'lláh, the Báb and 'Abdu'l-Bahá. Wilmette, IL: Baháí Publishing Trust, 2002.

Bahá'u'lláh. *Epistle to the Son of the Wolf*. Wilmette, IL: Baháí Publishing Trust, 1988.
— *Gleanings from the Writings of Bahá'u'lláh*. Wilmette, IL: Baháí Publishing Trust, 1983.
— *The Kitáb-i-Aqdas*. Haifa: Baháí World Centre, 1992.
— *Kitáb-i-Íqán*. Wilmette, IL: Baháí Publishing Trust, 1989.
— *Tablets of Bahá'u'lláh*. Wilmette, IL: Baháí Publishing Trust, 1988.

The Compilation of Compilations. Prepared by the Universal House of Justice 1963–1990. 2 vols. [Mona Vale NSW]: Baháí Publications Australia, 1991.

The Koran. Trans. J. M. Rodwell. London: Dent (Everyman's Library), 1963.

McReynolds, David. *Philosophy of Nonviolence*. Accessed at http://www.nonviolence.org/issues/philosophy-nonviolence.php

Prayers, Tablets, Instructions and Miscellany, Gathered by American Visitors to the Holy City During the Summer of 1900. Accessed at *Ocean* http://www.bahai-education.org/ocean/.

Shoghi Effendi. *Baháí Administration*. Wilmette, IL: Baháí Publishing Trust, 1968.

Star of the West. rpt. Oxford: George Ronald, 1984.

Taherzadeh, Adib. *The Revelation of Bahá'u'lláh*, vol. 1. Oxford: George Ronald, 1974.

The Universal House of Justice. Letter to an individual, 2 December 1985, in *Child Abuse, Psychology and Knowledge of Self*. Accessed at *Ocean* http://www.bahai-education.org/ocean/.